# Best Short Hikes in California's Northern Sierra

# Best Short Hikes in California's Northern Sierra

## A Guide to Day Hikes Near Campgrounds

• • • • • • • • • •

BY KAREN AND TERRY WHITEHILL

THE
MOUNTAINEERS

**THE MOUNTAINEERS**: Organized 1906 " . . . *to explore, study, preserve, and enjoy the natural beauty of the outdoors."*

First printing 1990, second printing 1992, third printing 1995, fourth printing 1998

Published by The Mountaineers
1001 SW Klickitat Way, Suite 201, Seattle, Washington 98134
Manufactured in the United States of America

Edited by Dana Fos
Maps by Nick Gregoric
Cover photograph Green Lake Canyon. Photo by Terry Whitehill
All photographs by the authors
Cover design by Barbara Bash
Book design by Barbara Bash
Frontispiece: Hearty hikers ascend the slopes of towering Mount Dana.
Page 5: Crown Point rules the skyline above Barney Lake.

**Library of Congress Cataloging in Publication Data**

Whitehill, Karen, 1957-
    Best short hikes in California's northern Sierra / by Karen and
Terry Whitehill.
        p. cm.
    Includes bibliographical references and index.
    ISBN 0-89886-255-8
    1. Hiking--Sierra Nevada Mountains (Calif. and Nev.)--Guide-books.
2. Sierra Nevada Mountains (Calif. and Nev.)--Description and travel--Guide-books.
I. Whitehill, Terry, 1954-
II. Mountaineers (Society) III. Title.
GV 199.42.S55W48 1990
917.94'4--dc20                                                    90-37686
                                                                  CIP

*For our daughter Sierra Jo —*

*May you always see creation
with the wonder of a child.*

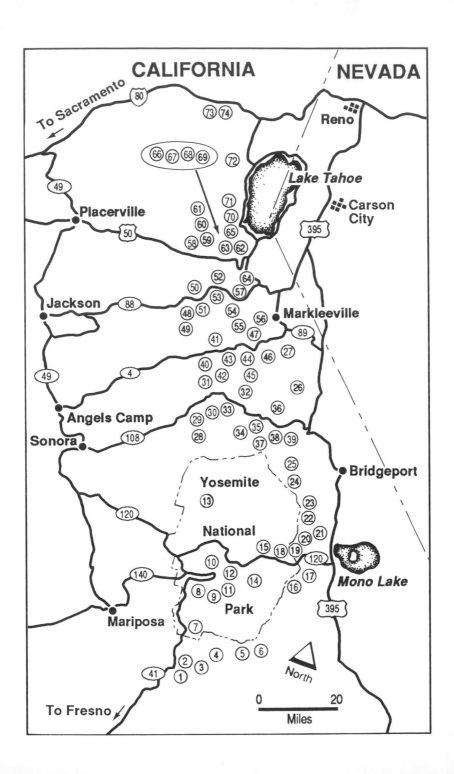

# • • • • • • • •
# Contents

*The trail toward Round Top is full of scenic pleasures.*

# INTRODUCTION
· · · · · · · · ·
# The Northern Sierra Nevada

The Sierra Nevada Mountains are California's best-loved inland playground. Each weekend, thousands of harried city dwellers make the multi-hour exodus by car from Los Angeles, San Francisco, and other urban centers, hoping to escape city life and find relaxation in the rugged serenity of the Sierra Nevada. These restless thousands gather in scores of easily accessible public campgrounds, unfurl their tents, level out their camper units, and settle in for a few days or weeks of uncivilized bliss. And just beyond their leaping campfires, a treasure trove of trails awaits them, beckoning toward gemlike lakes, flower-carpeted alpine meadows, and unmatched mountain vistas.

This book, *Best Short Hikes in California's Northern Sierra*, is the key with which the casual hiker can unlock the treasure of the Sierra Nevada. The volume's focus is on short hikes—"day" hikes for the nonbackpacker and easy weekend trips for those who want to carry in a pack and set up camp. The great majority of the 74 hikes described here are less than 10 miles long; many are less than 5 miles. All are situated in the northern Sierra Nevada (between the San Joaquin/Mammoth area and Donner Pass), and all offer scenic "perks," such as alpine lakes or meadows, spreading vistas, and wildflower extravaganzas.

This book really isn't written for all those gung-ho outdoorsmen who set off into the Sierra Nevada wilderness for long periods of time, intent on logging dozens of miles per day. Instead, it's written for the casual weekend hiker, for the family with young children, for the fisherman in search of a tempting stream, or for the older walker who doesn't want to carry 40 pounds of camping gear 15 miles to a lake.

A few of the hikes described here might be too difficult for some of the people who use this book. Other hikes might seem too easy for the majority of our audience. But with 74 hikes to choose from, anyone who brings this volume along on a trek to the Sierra Nevada will find a delightful overabundance of tempting excursions to sample.

## SIERRA HISTORY

The Sierra Nevada Mountains were the last great land barrier faced by weary pioneers as they made their westward journey toward the Pacific paradise called California. And what an awesome barrier those mountains presented. Stretching from south to north in a seemingly impenetrable wall of stone and ice, the Sierra Nevada Mountains soar as high as 14,494 feet at the summit of Mount Whitney, and the snowy passes that snake across them range in height from 7,000 to more than 9,000 feet.

The Sierra Nevada have been carved by three great forces over the span of several thousand years. First, volcanic action buried the area under thousands of feet of lava, mudflows, and volcanic sediment. Then, mighty glaciers etched out canyons and lakes, shoved up rocky ridges, and scaped away topsoil to leave bare granite. Finally, the undefeatable power of time itself left its imprint on the mountains, sculpting the rock with wind and rain to produce the masterpiece of nature we call the Sierra Nevada.

Native North American Indians have lived in and around these mountains for many centuries. Tribes such as the Washoe, Piute, Maidu, and Miwok left their footprints on the Sierra crest. The arrival of the white man came much later, with the first documented crossing of the Sierra by a white man dating back to 1826 and the trapper Jedediah Smith. Emigrants followed on the heels of the mountain men, and the Bartleson-Bidwell party became the first emigrant group to cross the Sierra in 1841. Behind that courageous vanguard came a flood of settlers, miners, and businessmen. Rough roads were built, then better ones—today, thousands of travelers cross and recross the Sierra every summer day.

## SIERRA VEGETATION

Wildflowers are one of the sweetest aspects of summer hiking in the Sierra Nevada. Once you've seen an alpine meadow awash in Lemmon's paintbrush and tiny elephant heads, or once you've watched a Sierra stream dance down a hillside covered with brilliant yellow monkeyflowers and tower larkspur, or once you've hiked across a mountain slope, alone but for the singing voices of alpine gold and pussypaws, you'll never forget the beauty of summer in the Sierra.

Sierra wildflowers are both abundant and amazingly diverse. If you'll be spending any time in the mountains at all, plan to invest in a flower book. Somehow, being able to give one of these tiny blossoms a name makes its beauty even more a part of you. Of course, you should never pick Sierra wildflowers, but you can take them home in photographs and in your growing knowledge of their wonderful variety.

Flowers aren't the only growing thing you'll have to learn about in the Sierra. These mountains also boast a tantalizing assortment of trees and bushes. As with the wildflowers, we've noted common trailside varieties with all the hike descriptions. This should help you in your identification efforts, but if you're really interested in becoming a Sierra vegetation expert, you'll probably want to invest in a tree book specific to the area (see Further Reading).

If you're not ready to begin toting extra books and spending a lot of money on your budding botany career, make use of the free handouts provided in all Forest Service offices. The Forest Service offers many well-written, informative flyers on Sierra trees and flowers, at no charge to the public.

## SIERRA ANIMALS

You'll see a lot of life-forms that aren't rooted to the ground during your time in the Sierra, ranging in size from tiny lodgepole chipmunks to graceful mule deer. Again, Forest Service flyers can help you learn the difference between Douglas squirrels and golden-mantled ground squirrels or Clark's nutcrackers and Steller's jays. But if you have a special interest, you may want to invest in a specific guidebook.

**Bears**. Every hiker should know about Sierra animals and be aware of personal safety procedures in the wilderness. Of course, everyone's first concern in the Sierra involves the infamous black bear. Will you see one while you're hiking? Probably not. As a day hiker with a limited food supply, you'll be much less attractive to pilfering black bears than the granola-laden backpackers who often visit the bears' domain. On the other hand, if you're staying at a campground during your Sierra visit, it's very possible that you'll see a bear—or at least awake to the sound of its passage on a late-night raid.

Scavenging bears have become an increasingly serious problem in the Sierra over recent years, especially in Yosemite National Park. The problem is compounded by people's carelessness. If you want to avoid a confrontation with a bear, use common sense with your food supply. Don't leave groceries on your campground picnic table, and don't take food into your tent at night. If your campsite has a metal bear box for food storage, use it. Otherwise, lock your foodstuffs in your car.

Not only do black bears know what a camper's dinner smells like, they know what it looks like, too. A well-educated raiding bear can spot a cooler through the window of a car—and he'll do his best to get it. Cover groceries and coolers with a blanket if they're visible through car windows, and don't ever leave garbage

*Mule deer are frequently seen along Sierra trails.*

or leftovers outside. And if by chance you should forget all these instructions one evening, and you wake up to find a bear consuming your last chocolate bar, remember the one all-important rule of bear relations. Possession is proof of ownership. Wish the bear *bon appétit* and never, never argue.

**Bugs**.   A much smaller Sierra pest is one you'll almost certainly encounter. Mosquitoes are abundant in the Sierra Nevada, especially when the ground is damp from the receding snows. June and July are usually the worst months for mosquito haters. Unfortunately, they're also two of the best months for wildflower watchers and those in quest of blissful summer weather.

Fight the buzzing hordes with light cotton clothing, long sleeves, and long pants. Arm yourself with gobs of mosquito repellent, and don't forget to dab your ankles and your wrists. A bandana tied around the neck and face will sometimes help, and a wide-brimmed hat will protect your forehead and scalp. Do what you can to win the battle with the little beasties, but you might as well accept this fact—bloodshed is simply unavoidable.

Ticks are yet another tiny pest that the Sierra may introduce to you on your visit. Although ticks are generally rare above 6,000 feet, it's best to expect the unexpected and be on your guard. Ticks like to hang out on bushes and tall grass, then hitch a ride with passing hikers. They usually find a moist, hairy place on the body, then dig in for dinner. Be sure to do a "tick check" at the end of every low-elevation Sierra hiking day. Comb or brush your hair thoroughly, and do a visual check on every inch of skin. Finally, examine your clothes and bedding for stowaways.

If you do find a tick that has already embedded itself in your skin, it must be removed completely to avoid infection. Tweezers may work if the tick isn't in too deep. If the area around the bite is already inflamed and sore, indicating that the tick has been with you for awhile, you may want to consult a doctor. Be sure to cleanse the wound thoroughly once the tick is out.

Some Sierra ticks are disease carriers, and the tick-induced Lyme disease is an increasing problem. If you experience any unusual symptoms after a tick encounter, make a beeline for a doctor.

**Snakes.**   One more concern with Sierra hiking has to do with rattlesnakes. Fortunately, rattlesnakes are seldom seen above 8,000 feet, and they're actually quite rare above the 6,000- or 7,000-foot level. Most of the hikes in this volume are well above the range of rattlesnakes. On the lower hikes (the one at Hetch Hetchy Reservoir, for example), you can lessen your chances of a snake encounter by being alert, keeping to the trail, and staying out of rocks, brush, and grass.

**Pack animals.**   Some friendlier and much larger beasts you're almost sure to meet on Sierra trails are the sturdy horses and mules that serve as the area's long-haul truckers. You'll probably encounter long lines of pack animals transporting gear and groceries for groups of paying customers, especially in Yosemite National Park. And you'll probably see many individuals in smaller groups exploring the Sierra on their own mounts. No matter what your feelings on the pros and cons of horses in the wilderness, the fact of the matter is, they're there to stay. Follow some simple rules for peaceful coexistence, and you'll make life more pleasant for both two-legged and four-legged Sierra travelers.

If you're approached or overtaken by pack animals on a Sierra trail, always yield the right-of-way. It's much easier for a hiker to scramble into the underbrush or climb onto a log than it is for a skittish horse or mule to move aside. For your own safety, always escape to the uphill side of the trail if you're being passed on a steep grade. Avoid loud noises or flamboyant gestures while the animals go by. Their riders usually have their hands full enough on rough Sierra trails. Startled horses or mules can be very dangerous.

## HIKING AND SAFETY

And what does the Sierra Nevada promise the traveler of today? Pristine alpine lakes for fishing and swimming, rugged mountain trails for solitary wandering, glorious far-reaching vistas that remain unspoiled across the centuries— these are just a few of its attractions. But, just as the emigrants of the nineteenth century learned to venture into the Sierra armed with caution and respect, today's foot traveler must also respect the mountains he explores. And he must take precautions to ensure his journey is a safe one.

**Solitude**.   To begin with, never set out alone on a Sierra trail without letting someone know of your hiking plans. If you're using a trailhead that doesn't have a hikers' register (most don't), it's a good idea to notify a Forest Service office or a campground host of your intended route, destination, and return time.

**Supplies**.   Always carry the Ten Essentials: a map, extra clothing, matches, a knife, a compass in case you lose your way or leave the trail for cross-country scrambling, a flashlight, some form of fire-starter (for starting a fire with wet wood), a first aid kit, sunglasses, and an emergency food supply. And don't forget one more essential of summer hiking in the Sierra Nevada—sunscreen.

**Water**.   Unfortunately, many Sierra streams and lakes are now polluted with *Giardia*. Heavy cattle grazing and irresponsible wilderness users multiply the problem with each new hiking season. If you want to be absolutely sure you don't experience the distress of giardiasis (severe diarrhea and stomach cramps), don't drink anything but treated water. Day hikers should be able to carry all the liquids they require. Backpackers may want to utilize a water filter or a chemical treatment system. Otherwise, water must be boiled at least 5 minutes to make it safe.

**Weather**.   Just as you can't predict the drinkability of a sparkling Sierra stream, neither can you predict the longevity of a clear Sierra sky. Mountain weather is notoriously changeable, and a Sierra

*Storms brew up quickly in the Sierra; when lightning starts, take cover!*

summer day can go from sun and balmy temperatures to flashing lightning and a torrential downpour in less time than you'll have to hike back to your car.

Always carry a jacket or a windbreaker on Sierra trails, no matter how lovely the morning dawns. And never linger on an exposed ridge when thunderclouds begin to gather. Don't take chances with your life—head for lower ground. Lightning strikes often in the Sierra. Take a look at one of the charcoal-black snags that stand on every Sierra ridgetop, and you'll be reminded of the destructive power of this seemingly mild climate.

**Routefinding.**   The majority of the trails described here are well defined and easy to follow. But some trails cut across bare slabs of granite or get such little use that they can be overgrown. Be aware of the clues you need to watch for as you try to find your way. "Blazes" are shallow cuts made into the trunks of trees, usually at eye level or above, to indicate a trail's correct route. Blazes can also be splashes of bright paint left on trees or boulders along the way.

"Cairns" are large piles of stones, often waist height or even higher, used as easy-to-spot markers when a trail crosses barren ground. Cairns often decorate ridgetops, mountain summits, and the opposite banks on river crossings. "Ducks" are smaller versions of rock cairns, sometimes consisting of only a few flat stones piled one atop another. Often, hundreds of tiny ducks are perched pre-cariously beside a trail, pointing out a route that weaves through a granite landscape where footprints leave no mark.

Yet another method of trail marking involves outlining a route with a line of stones or logs. Again, you'll often see this when a trail crosses a shelf of granite or a scree-covered alpine slope.

**Footwear.**   Because the Sierra Nevada consists of many vast ex-panses of open granite and sharp-edged glacial rubble, trail surfaces are often rough and unstable. If you're prone to turned ankles and/or bruised insteps, you'll definitely want to hike in ankle-high boots with sturdy soles. If you prefer a more light-footed approach to mountain wandering, a pair of waffle-soled running or walking shoes will probably suffice (assuming the absence of winter snows). The choice is yours.

## HOW TO USE THIS BOOK

The 74 hike descriptions that follow are arranged geographically, working from south to north and from west to east. Each geographi-cal section centers around a major highway (e.g., Carson Pass, Sonora Pass, Ebbetts Pass). And each section is preceded by a brief introduction with information specific to that area.

*"Ducks" mark the rugged and rocky Sierra trails.*

**Information blocks.**   Preliminary information for each hike covers such topics as distance and difficulty (rated "easy," "moderate," or "strenuous"). A starting point and a high point are also provided for each hike. If a hike's total elevation gain is significantly greater than the difference between its starting point and high point, a figure is given for total climb as well.

**Maps.**   As mentioned in the "Hiking and Safety" section, it's important to have a good map along on all excursions. Each hike described in this book is accompanied by a small route map, but you'll also want to carry an overall area map to help you keep your bearings and to aid in identifying distant peaks and lakes.

For those in quest of a lot of detail, a United States Geological Survey (USGS) quadrangle map is listed for each hike in this volume. These maps are very good, but they do have their drawbacks. Some have not been updated since the 1950s, and most are at least 10 years old. Roads and trails do change, so be sure to check your map against the book's hike map whenever there's a question.

If you're hiking in several scattered areas, quadrangle maps can be expensive and somewhat difficult to obtain. If you're willing to settle for a larger scale view of your surroundings, excellent, inexpensive maps are available at Forest Service offices for each area covered in this volume. The Forest Service has wonderful maps of both the Hoover Wilderness and the Emigrant Wilderness.

When ordering maps from the Forest Service, it is important to give them the exact name. We've listed exact map names in the information blocks. Sometimes the word "Reservoir" is spelled out, sometimes it is abbreviated to "Res."

**Trip descriptions**.  Think of this volume's 74 hikes and their information blocks as a varied and extensive menu placed before you—a hungry, eager hiker. Now, how do you decide which dish to sample? Of course, such factors as the hike's location, length, and elevation gain will figure heavily into your decision. But, just as you can't be sure what a particular menu offering is really like until you coax a bit of an elaboration from your waiter, you won't really know this volume's hikes until you dig into the trip descriptions.

That's where you'll learn about each trip's delights. Will you be hiking to a lake, a mountaintop, or a windswept ridge? Will you see wildflowers, waterfalls, or towering firs? Will the trail be rough and rocky or carpeted with pine needles? The descriptions warn you about steep pitches, tempt you with breathtaking vistas, and lure you on with promises of icy brooks. First, whet your appetite. Then, experience the twists and turns and junctions. Finally, step back and feast your senses.

**When to go**.  Because weather conditions in the Sierra Nevada can and do vary greatly from one year to the next, this book avoids predictions of when certain hikes will be open for snow-free exploration. Be advised that the Sierra's winter snowpack will dictate your summer hiking schedule. In a heavy snow year, many of the high-elevation hikes listed in this volume are not completely free of snow until early or mid-August. In fact, some shaded sections of the higher trails may never escape the grasp of winter. In a light snow year, even the loftiest trails may be open by July 1.

Utilize the starting point and high point figures for each hike to help you gauge your chances of following the receding snow line upward. Whatever you do, don't rush it. Steeply sloped snow-fields are extremely treacherous to cross. Never attempt to negotiate a snow-covered section of trail if you are inexperienced or if you're hiking alone.

The best way to find out if a particular trail is open is to phone the local ranger station or stop and ask on your way in. Forest Service personnel will be able to provide you with information on the current trail conditions and recommendations on alternate trails, if needed. If the snow is lingering, choose one of the Sierra's many lower-elevation hikes instead, and save your loftier excursions for a little later in the year. Besides the safety factor, hiking across vast snowfields entails another disadvantage. It means you've come too early for the flowers.

**Camping.** Because many outdoor lovers like to combine their hiking trips with camping excursions, every one of this book's nine hike groupings is accompanied by a listing of convenient campgrounds. Information on fees, reservations, and facilities is given for each campground, and an approximate number of sites per campground is provided when possible. Please keep in mind that these figures can change; Sierra campgrounds seem to undergo continual evolution.

Camping in the Sierra Nevada is an inexpensive and rewarding alternative to staying in hotels or inns. Besides, indoor accommodations are extremely limited on most Sierra passes, and when available they're far from cheap. Campgrounds in the Sierra range from moderately priced, private establishments situated in resort areas near lakes or streams to secluded, primitive sites with limited facilities, no fees, and oftentimes no drinking water.

Forest Service campgrounds are plentiful and diverse in the Sierra. Most don't accept reservations, although there are exceptions (especially in Yosemite National Park and the area around Lake Tahoe). Some have resident campground hosts, available to answer questions and collect camping fees. Others have very little supervision and require self-payment at a drop box near the campground entrance.

Generally, you'll be able to find an open site in the Sierra on summer weekdays and early Friday afternoons. Friday evenings can be frenzied, and on Saturdays, campgrounds are sometimes overflowing with tents and trailer units. New rules apply if you are planning to camp in Yosemite National Park. You'll always need reservations in Yosemite Valley. Tioga Pass can be tough as well.

Sierra Nevada campground reservations are most widely obtained through Ticketron or through the Forest Service's designated representative. You can visit Ticketron outlets in person or write to Ticketron Reservations, PO Box 2715, San Francisco,

California 94126. To obtain reservations for Forest Service campgrounds, call (800) 280-2267 (CAMP).

If you don't have a favorite campground or a prior reservation, always stop at the local Forest Service office on your way into the mountains. You can pick up a free listing of area campgrounds with information on size, facilities, and fees at any Forest Service office. And, if you're unfamiliar with the sites available, you should be able to coax a campground recommendation from the person behind the desk.

As mentioned earlier, each of the nine hike groupings in this volume is accompanied by a list of convenient campgrounds, the majority of which do not require reservations. If you'd like even more input on the subject, consider purchasing a campground guide. One source we've found extremely helpful throughout our stay in the Sierra is *California Camping, the Complete Guide to California's Recreation Areas*, by Tom Stienstra (Foghorn Press). This book lists more than 1,500 campgrounds, with details on facilities, fees, locations, and nearby recreation opportunities. It also boasts an introductory section with useful hints on equipment, cooking, first aid, etc.

Another camping option you should be aware of is the practice of "free camping" on Forest Service land. This is legal and acceptable, providing the land is Forest Service property and there is no posting of "no camping" signs. Some drawbacks to this practice include lack of facilities (no water, no toilets), limited security, and possible impact to the environment. Also, if fire restrictions are in effect because of dry conditions, you won't be able to enjoy a crackling campfire (or a toasted marshmallow).

If you do choose to free camp in the forest, please be a responsible wilderness user. Drive your vehicle only on established roadways. Carry out all your trash, and clean out your firepit. Burn your toilet paper, and always dispose of human waste by digging a 6- to 8-inch hole, at least 50 yards away from any water source.

## A REMINDER

The Sierra Nevada Mountains are a treasure waiting to be discovered. Use this book to unlock the riches of this wilderness. Walk safely and softly while you visit. And leave the mountains as you found them, unspoiled and untamable, awaiting the footsteps of another generation.

# A NOTE ABOUT SAFETY

Safety is an important concern in all outdoor activities. No guidebook can alert you to every hazard or anticipate the limitations of every reader. Therefore, the descriptions of roads, trails, routes, and natural features in this book are not representations that a particular place or excursion will be safe for your party. When you follow any of the routes described in this book, you assume responsibility for your own safety. Under normal conditions, such excursions require the usual attention to traffic, road and trail conditions, weather, terrain, the capabilities of your party, and other factors. Keeping informed on current conditions and exercising common sense are the keys to a safe, enjoyable outing.

*The Mountaineers*

*Heavily laden backpackers descend from The Niche, 8,000 feet.*

# CHAPTER ONE

• • • • • • • • •

# Yosemite South

The San Joaquin River forms a natural dividing line between the northern and southern Sierra Nevada, with the mountainous area just north of the San Joaquin and just south of Yosemite National Park offering a diverse mix of high- and low-elevation hikes. Within this area is the Ansel Adams Wilderness, covering more than 200,000 acres and ascending to a lofty 13,157 feet at the summit of Mount Ritter.

Formerly called the Minarets Wilderness, the Ansel Aaams Wilderness boasts scores of rugged granite mountains, several large lakes, and many small glaciers on its highest peaks. Wilderness permits are required for overnight trips in the area, but day hikers are allowed to enter the Wilderness without permits.

For those entering the Wilderness from the west, overnight permits can be obtained at the Minarets Ranger District Office in North Fork. The mailing address is Sierra National Forest, Minarets Ranger District, North Fork, California 93643. Those approaching from the east can claim overnight permits at the Forest Service office at Mammoth Lakes. To contact the office by mail, write to Inyo National Forest, Mammoth Ranger District, Mammoth Lakes, California 93546.

The tourist hub of the southern Yosemite area is the speedboat-tormented Bass Lake. Bass Lake boasts several developed (and crowded) campgrounds, all requiring reservations. There's a convenient Forest Service office on Highway 41, just north of the town of Oakhurst. Here the office staff assists a steady flow of visitors with wilderness and campfire permits, area maps, and information.

## CAMPGROUNDS

**Grey's Mountain Campground** (*Hike 2, Shadow of the Giants; Hike 3, Bull Buck Trail; Hike 4, Fresno Dome*) Rustic Grey's Mountain Campground is a favorite with families and bargain-seeking campers. There are approximately 20 tentsites in this free campground,

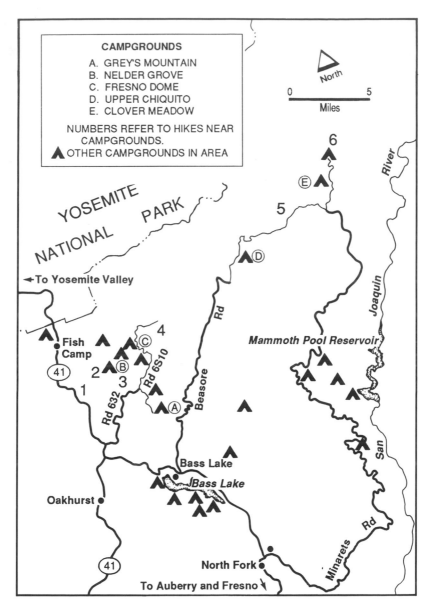

CAMPGROUNDS

A. GREY'S MOUNTAIN
B. NELDER GROVE
C. FRESNO DOME
D. UPPER CHIQUITO
E. CLOVER MEADOW

NUMBERS REFER TO HIKES NEAR
CAMPGROUNDS.
▲ OTHER CAMPGROUNDS IN AREA

North

0        5
Miles

YOSEMITE NATIONAL PARK

← To Yosemite Valley

Fish Camp

Mammoth Pool Reservoir

Rd

Rd 6S10

Rd 632

Beasore

Joaquin

San

Bass Lake

Bass Lake

Oakhurst

Minarets Rd

North Fork

To Auberry and Fresno ↓

nestled beside pleasant Willow Creek. Grey's Mountain Campground also boasts a wonderful swimming hole, just downstream from the camping area.

Reach the campground by driving 4.1 miles north from Oakhurst on Highway 41. Turn off onto paved Road 632, signed as Sky Ranch Road. This becomes Road 6S10. Pass the turnoff for Nelder Grove Campground, then turn right at the sign for Soquel

Campground. Take the rough, unpaved road past Soquel Campground and reach Grey's Mountain Campground 9.0 miles from Highway 41.

Shaded by firs and incense cedars, sites offer picnic tables, fireplaces, and non-flush toilets. There is no drinking water, so you'll want to fill up at Oakhurst on your way in. The campground is open June to November. No reservations. Moderate fee.

**Nelder Grove Campground** *(Hike 1, Lewis Creek Trail; Hike 2, Shadow of the Giants; Hike 3, Bull Buck Trail; Hike 4, Fresno Dome)* This wonderful campground provides a unique opportunity to pitch your tent or park your trailer among massive giant sequoia stumps, the leftovers of a long-ceased logging operation. Its 10 campsites for tents or motorhomes occupy a pleasant, shaded spot, nestled beside dainty California Creek. A 1.0-mile trail along the little waterway winds past several living giant sequoia trees. Hike 3 leaves right from the campground, too.

Nelder Grove Campground is 12.0 miles northeast of Oakhurst. Turn off Highway 41 onto Road 632, signed as Sky Ranch Road. This becomes Road 6S10. Turn left at the sign for Shadow of the Giants and Nelder Grove Campground, then go right at the next junction and watch for the campground on the left after about a mile.

Be sure to stop at the entrance to talk with volunteer ranger John Hawksworth. Hawksworth has worked summers at the campground for more than a decade, and he'll be glad to guide you through his exhibit on the Sugar Pine logging operation. Afterwards, find a shaded campspot among the sequoia stumps. Sites have fireplaces and picnic tables. There are non-flush toilets but there's no drinking water. Nelder Grove Campground is open May to October. No reservations. No fee.

**Fresno Dome Campground** *(Hike 4, Fresno Dome)* The secluded Fresno Dome Campground is well worth the drive from Highway 41, especially if you're planning to make the scramble to the summit of Fresno Dome. Its 12 sites (6 for tents, 6 for motorhomes) are adjacent to petite Big Creek, and lovely meadows are nearby.

Drive 4.1 miles north from Oakhurst on Highway 41 and turn off onto Road 632, signed as Sky Ranch Road. This becomes Road 6S10. Stay on the paved 6S10 to Kelty Meadows, then lose the pavement as you follow signs for Fresno Dome Campground (still on 6S10). Reach a junction and keep left to reach the campground, 12.3 miles from Highway 41.

There is no drinking water here, so you'll want to fill up at Oakhurst on your way in. Sites offer picnic tables and fireplaces. Non-flush toilets are available. The campground is open June to November. No reservations. Moderate fee.

**Upper Chiquito Campground** *(Hike 5, Lower Jackass Lake)* The shaded Upper Chiquito Campground has more than 20 sites (some for tents, some for motorhomes) strung out along Chiquito Creek, an exceedingly popular spot for fishermen. The campground is sprawling and dusty, but it offers convenient access to Hike 5, and nearby Globe Rock (the rock is 1.0 mile southwest of the campground, just off Beasore Road).

Globe Rock is a playfully perched "glacial erratic," a traveling boulder left behind by a departing glacier. This massive hunk of rock sits atop a narrow stone base of softer rock, eroded by time and nature into a precarious pedestal. Globe Rock is well signed, and there's an informational plaque at the site.

Reach Upper Chiquito Campground via Oakhurst on Highway 41. From Oakhurst, drive north 3.5 miles to Yosemite Forks, and turn onto Road 222 toward Bass Lake. Gain the unpaved Beasore Road at the north end of Bass Lake, and follow it for 16.0 miles to the campground. Campsites are 0.5 mile off the road.

There's a summer ranger living at Upper Chiquito Campground. Picnic tables and fireplaces are provided, but there's no drinking water. Upper Chiquito Campground is open June to October. No reservations. No fee.

**Clover Meadow Campground** *(Hike 6, Cora Lake)* You can reach Clover Meadow Campground from North Fork (south of Oakhurst and Bass Lake) via the paved but narrow and winding Minarets Road. From North Fork, follow signs for Mammoth Pool. It's a scenic but slow 54-mile drive to Clover Meadow Campground.

Be sure to watch for the signed Mile High Vista along the way. This viewpoint/picnic area just off the Minarets Road offers restrooms and picnic tables, as well as a breathtaking look down onto Mammoth Pool Reservoir. On a clear day, there's an awesome panorama of the Ritter Range, with Mount Ritter, the Minarets, and Mammoth Mountain all visible. You'll do well to postpone your lunch until you reach the lofty picnic spot—the twisting Minarets Road will challenge even the most hearty stomach.

If you're willing to brave a shorter, unpaved route to Clover Meadow Campground, take Beasore Road from the north end of Bass Lake (see directions for Upper Chiquito Campground). It's 30.0 miles to the junction with Minarets Road. Drive north an additional 2.0 miles to reach the campground. You'll pass a staffed ranger station as you enter.

Seven sites for tents or motorhomes offer picnic tables, fireplaces, water, and non-flush toilets, and the surrounding wildflower meadows are filled with clover, crimson columbine, and shooting star. Clover Meadow Campground is open June to October. No reservations. Moderate fee.

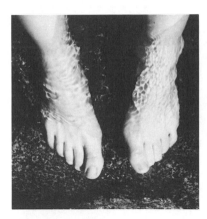

## • • • • • • • • • • •
# 1 LEWIS CREEK TRAIL

Distance: 3.4 miles round trip
Difficulty: Easy
Starting point: 4,060 feet
High point: 4,200 feet
Map: USGS Bass Lake 15'

*A hiker cools her toes in Lewis Creek.*

This hike along a portion of the scenic Lewis Creek Trail leads to pretty Red Rock Falls, a fine goal for an easy family outing and a "picnic-perfect" destination. You can add a second waterfall to your day by making the 0.2-mile round-trip jaunt to lovely Corlieu Falls, the highest waterfall in Madera County.

One warning about the Lewis Creek Trail, however—the lower section (below Corlieu Falls) often harbors an abundance of poison oak. So be on the lookout!

Camping options near the trail are abundant. There are several reservation campgrounds on the Bass Lake shoreline, and the Grey's Mountain and Nelder Grove campgrounds aren't too far away.

To reach the trailhead, drive north from Oakhurst on Highway 41. Proceed 4.0 miles north of the Bass Lake junction, and watch for a 4,000-foot elevation road marker. Next, you'll pass a sign announcing "Turnout to allow passing—200 feet." Park in the large, gravel turnout just beyond. There's a trailhead sign for the Lewis Creek Trail here.

Descend from the parking area on an unpaved road and reach a signed junction soon after. Continue straight for Red Rock Falls, noting the 0.1-mile trail leaving to the right that leads downstream to Corlieu Falls. (You may want to add this to your day, if you have the time. Corlieu Falls is quite impressive.)

The route to Red Rock Falls winds on beneath a canopy of incense cedars, then crosses Lewis Creek on a sturdy footbridge. Continue gently uphill with the trail. The strong aroma of mountain misery will keep you company in early summer, and the song of Lewis Creek will be the backdrop to your footsteps as you hike.

Early season flowers are abundant here. Watch for western pennyroyal, pale pink Dudley's Clarkia, and bright yellow common madia. Sweet-smelling spearmint is another trailside treat. Cross a branch of Lewis Creek at 0.3 mile and continue in the shade of

*Exquisite tiger lilies prowl the banks of little Lewis Creek.*

incense cedars and tall white firs, climbing gently toward Red Rock Falls.

The creek boasts a score of tempting pools to tantalize hot toes. Cross an inlet creek on a small footbridge at 0.7 mile, and watch for western azaleas along the trail. The banks of Lewis Creek are bright with foxglove and tiger lily, and the forest is a pleasant mix of Sierra alders, wild filberts, creek dogwoods, and the ever-present incense cedars. Watch for an occasional ponderosa pine or sugar pine as well.

Arrive at a junction at 1.7 miles, and angle left for Red Rock Falls. A short descent leads to this pretty nook where the waters of Lewis Creek slip over a bench of silky-smooth, red-hued rock, tumbling about 15 feet to the creekbed below. Cool pools for wading and flat rocks for picnicking will make your stay a pleasant one, but be sure to keep small children under supervision near the dropoff.

Retrace your steps to regain your starting point, or add the jaunt to Corlieu Falls if you're in the mood for another lovely waterfall.

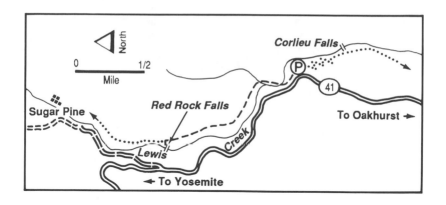

## 2 SHADOW OF THE GIANTS NATIONAL RECREATION TRAIL

Distance: 1.2 miles (loop)
Difficulty: Easy
Starting point: 5,300 feet
High point: 5,400 feet
Map: USGS Bass Lake 15'

This charming, easy trail winds along Nelder Creek, wandering through an impressive scattering of giant sequoias sure to impress all who come to visit. If you're hiking with children, this is one excursion you won't want to miss. The walk is educational, entertaining, and relatively effortless, possessing all the characteristics of a successful family outing.

You can drive to the trailhead for this hike from either Grey's Mountain Campground or Nelder Grove Campground. From Oakhurst, drive 4.1 miles north on Highway 41 and turn off onto Road 632, signed as Sky Ranch Road. This becomes Road 6S10. Turn left at the sign for Shadow of the Giants and Nelder Grove Campground, then go left at the next junction and drive 0.5 mile to reach the trailhead. It's 11.5 miles from Oakhurst.

There are toilets available at the trail's start, and you'll want to allow 45 minutes to an hour for the walk, even though it's only 1.2 miles. The many informational plaques along the route are worth long study, as are the majestic forms of the giant sequoias that cast their shadows on a more humble forest of incense cedars, sugar pines, and white firs.

The trail splits soon after it begins. Take the branch to the left so you'll work through the informational plaques in their logical order. Climb very gently beside Nelder Creek, pausing to learn about native trees, shrubs, and animals as you go.

Cross the quiet waterway at the halfway point, then enjoy an easy downhill cruise to regain the parking area and starting point.

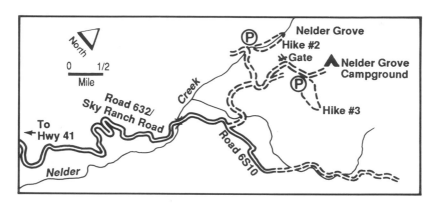

## 3   BULL BUCK TRAIL

Distance: 0.75 mile (loop)
Difficulty: Easy
Starting point: 5,300 feet
High point: 5,400 feet
Map: USGS Bass Lake 15'

This trail makes a delightful short outing, especially if you're staying at Nelder Grove Campground or the nearby Grey's Mountain Campground. It's an easy, pleasant walk to the base of the Bull Buck Tree, famed as one of the largest trees in the world. Tucked away in the Nelder Grove of giant sequoias, the Bull Buck Tree measures 99 feet around, and its estimated age is 2,700 years.

To reach the trailhead, drive 4.1 miles north from Oakhurst and turn off Highway 41 onto Road 632, signed as Sky Ranch Road. This becomes Road 6S10. Turn left at the sign for Shadow of the Giants and Nelder Grove Campground, then go right at the next junction and watch for the campground on the left after about a mile.

Drive through the campground, cross California Creek, and park in the small picnic area just beyond. You'll see a signpost for the Bull Buck Trail at the edge of the picnic area. Take the trail to the right of the signpost to approach the tree from the most impressive angle. You'll return on the other leg of the 0.75-mile loop.

It's a gentle, short climb through the 1,540-acre Nelder Grove to the Bull Buck Tree. The Nelder Grove boasts 106 mature giant sequoias in an enchanting setting of sugar pines, white firs, and incense cedars. Massive giant sequoia stumps are the sad witnesses of the ravages of long-ceased logging operations. Luckily, though, the Bull Buck Tree was overlooked.

Linger in the shadow of this aged giant for a while, and imagine the centuries that have come and gone since it was but a seedling. Unlike many other types of trees, giant sequoias aren't eliminated by forest fires. Their amazingly tough bark resists even the fiercest flames, enabling them to attain long, long life spans.

If you're looking for a photo angle of this stocky fellow, the best spot for a shot of the Bull Buck is from a "photo lane" cut through the forest on the south side of the tree. Continue on along the loop trail to regain your starting point.

*The ancient Bull Buck Tree is an amazing forest giant.*

• • • • • • • • • • • • • • • • • • • • • • •

# 4 FRESNO DOME

Distance: 1.6 miles round trip
Difficulty: Moderate
Starting point: 7,000 feet
High point: 7,540 feet
Map: USGS Bass Lake 15'

For a moderately challenging climb and a wonderful perch on which to spread a picnic or view a sunset, try this hike to the top of Fresno Dome. Pack in a dinner, a jacket, and a flashlight, and you can linger long enough to watch the sun lose itself in the haze of the golden west.

The best access to this hike is from the nearby Fresno Dome Campground, although Grey's Mountain Campground and Nelder Grove Campground are also convenient options. To reach the Fresno Dome trailhead, drive 4.1 miles north from Oakhurst on Highway 41 and turn off onto Road 632, signed as Sky Ranch Road. This becomes Road 6S10. Stay on the paved 6S10 to Kelty Meadows, then lose the pavement as you follow signs for Fresno Dome Campground (still on 6S10). Reach a junction just before Fresno Dome Campground, and continue on Road 6S10 for another 2.8 miles to reach the turnoff for the Fresno Dome trailhead.

The trail takes off across a pleasant meadow, beginning with a gentle climb and ending with a steep pitch up a barren slope that

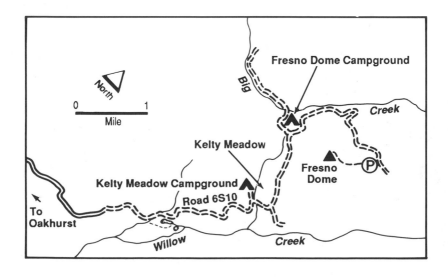

*A glowing sunset silhouettes a pine near the summit of Fresno Dome.*

culminates at the summit of Fresno Dome. Although the dome is rocky, the footing really isn't bad.

This is a "mountain climb" that even the most timid hiker will enjoy. And the view from the top is worth all the heavy breathing it takes to get there.

To the east, the Sierra ridgeline is a rugged wall of ice and granite. To the west, the San Joaquin Valley shimmers in the heat. And to the south, the lights of Fresno twinkle in the dusk that falls with evening. Pull up a rock and let your eyes savor the riches of Fresno Dome.

• • • • • • • • • • •

# 5 LOWER JACKASS LAKE

Distance: 4.6 miles round trip
Difficulty: Moderate
Starting point: 7,600 feet
High point: 8,600 feet
Map: USGS Merced Peak 15'

*Lofty Lower Jackass Lake offers a scenic, shaded shoreline.*

Although it's a short 2.3 miles to Lower Jackass Lake, don't sell this hike short. It offers lovely mountain views, pleasant forest hiking, and two lakeshores to linger on and explore. If you're camping, the trailhead for Lower Jackass Lake is a short drive from Upper Chiquito Campground.

To reach the trailhead, leave Oakhurst on Highway 41, and drive north 3.5 miles to Yosemite Forks, then turn onto Road 222 toward Bass Lake. Gain the unpaved Beasore Road at the north end of Bass Lake, and drive 29.0 miles to a turnoff signed "Norris Trailhead—2 miles." Drive in on the unpaved entry road and leave your vehicle in the parking area beside Norris Creek.

Take the creekside trail along the pretty waterway, winding through green meadows lush with wildflowers. Watch for fish hiding in the shadows cast by the lodgepole pines and red firs that stand above the water. Climb gently at first, then more steeply as you approach the boundary of the Ansel Adams Wilderness. Reach a wilderness sign at 1.0 mile.

Continue climbing steadily, and arrive at petite and shallow Norris Lake at 1.5 miles. Skirt to the right along the shore, following

*A young fisherman tests the waters of Granite Creek.*

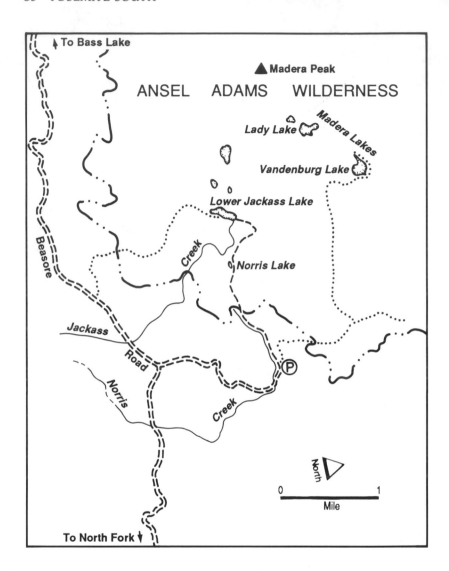

a well-defined trail. The terrain mellows for a quarter of a mile, then the climb resumes. Ascend steeply to gain a ridgeline with fine vistas of the mountains to the south and east.

Enjoy a panoramic view as you continue along the ridge, then descend slightly to reach the large, cliff-backed Lower Jackass Lake. Tucked into the Sierra landscape at a lofty 8,600 feet, Lower Jackass Lake is a watery gem offering excellent swimming and admirable picnic spots. Plan to linger for an hour and absorb the lakeside atmosphere.

• • • • • • • • • • • • • • • • • • • • • • • • • •

# 6 CORA LAKE

Distance: 9.0 miles round trip
Difficulty: Strenuous
Starting point: 7,000 feet
High point: 8,350 feet
Map: USGS Merced Peak 15'

Although it's fairly long, the hike to Cora Lake is not too difficult. Just allow yourself plenty of time to make the trek, and plan a leisurely rest/lunch break for the lake.

The trailhead for this hike can be gained with a brief drive from Clover Meadow Campground. Reach the trailhead from the little town of North Fork (south of Oakhurst and Bass Lake) via the paved but narrow and winding Minarets Road. From North Fork, follow signs for Mammoth Pool. It's a scenic but slow 54-mile drive to Clover Meadow Campground.

If you're willing to brave a shorter, unpaved route to Clover Meadow Campground, take Beasore Road from the north end of Bass Lake (see directions for Upper Chiquito Campground). It's 30.0 miles to the junction with Minarets Road. Drive north an additional 2.0 miles to reach the campground.

Pass the campground and Clover Meadow ranger station and branch right at the junction signed for Granite Creek Campground. The entry road to the campground and trailhead is unpaved, and it deteriorates markedly over the final 0.3 mile.

If you're not in a four-wheel-drive vehicle, you may want to park on the hill before the final steep descent to the campground and trailhead. Go left at the junction signed "Upper campground/ Soldier Meadow," and reach a parking area soon afterward.

Leave the parking area on foot and ford little Granite Creek. The way branches just beyond. Take the path to the right to gain the Isberg Trail. You'll cross a recently completed logging road at 0.5 mile. (Note: This may become an alternate starting point if the finished road is wide enough for parking cars.)

Continue climbing steadily through a forest of red firs and lodgepole pines. After the first 2.0 miles, the grade increases perceptibly. Another 0.5 mile of strenuous hiking will bring you to The Niche, 8,000 feet. You'll have fine views of the surrounding mountains as you approach the spot.

Enjoy more level walking along a pretty creek boasting tiger lilies, crimson columbine, lupine, Indian paintbrush, and lovely western azaleas. The little waterway offers a lot of inviting pools for toe wiggling and picnicking. Continue beside the creek and

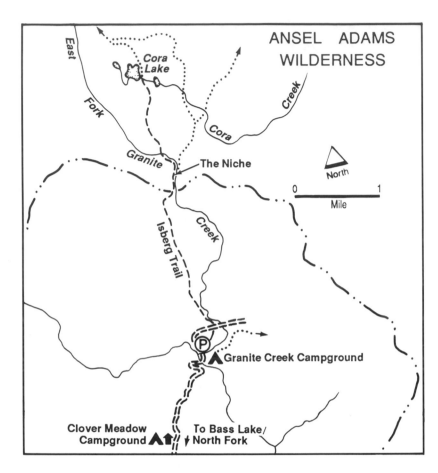

reach a sign for Cora Lake at the 3.0-mile point.

Go straight for Cora Lake. Cross the East Fork of Granite Creek at 3.3 miles, then climb more steeply for a while. Reach Cora Lake at 4.5 miles.

If you'd like to do more at Cora Lake than cool your toes or munch a sandwich, you can add 0.4 mile and a fine view by following the lakeside path to the left along the lakeshore. Watch for a large, exposed granite shelf on the right side of the trail after 0.1 mile. Veer left here to scramble up a small rocky butte.

The view from the top is worth the added effort, providing a vista to the northeast that includes Sadler Peak (on the left), Mount Ritter (in the middle), and the jagged tips of the Minarets (on the right), rearing skyward above the placid surface of Cora Lake.

# CHAPTER TWO

• • • • • • • •

# Yosemite Valley

The name "Yosemite" comes from the Indian tribe that inhabited the present-day Yosemite Valley before its discovery by the white man. The chief of this tribe, Teneiya (who lent his name to Tioga Pass's Tenaya Lake), led an unsuccessful resistance effort against the encroaching forces of the United States Army in the 1850s. The Mariposa Battalion, sent to roust Chief Teneiya from his mountain refuge, stumbled upon one of the most beautiful scenes in the entire Sierra Nevada—the soon-to-be-famous Yosemite Valley.

Although it's probable that the soldiers of the Mariposa Battalion weren't the first white men to explore the valley carved by the Merced River (a diary of William Penn Abrams records a visit there in 1849), it was the Mariposa Battalion that explored the wonders of Yosemite Valley and made those wonders known to the world. Less than forty years later, Yosemite became America's second national park.

One hundred years old, as of October 1990, Yosemite National Park stands with its predecessor, Yellowstone, as a foundation stone of America's national park system. Once threatened by overgrazing, logging, and exploitation, this matchless corner of American wilderness hung in the balance in the mid-nineteenth century. But men like John Muir, Galen Clark, John Conness, and Frederick Law Olmsted contributed their time and talents to the preservation of the land for future generations. And, on October 1, 1890, President Benjamin Harrison signed the legislation that made Yosemite a protected national treasure.

Today, the challenges of protection and preservation are still immense. More than 3 million people visit Yosemite Valley every year. The problems of traffic control, waste removal, and air pollution are pressing concerns. But the beauty that is Yosemite's remains unequalled in the 1990s, just as it was in the 1850s, and it is that beauty that makes hiking in Yosemite Valley worth the crowds, worth the regulations, and worth the hassles.

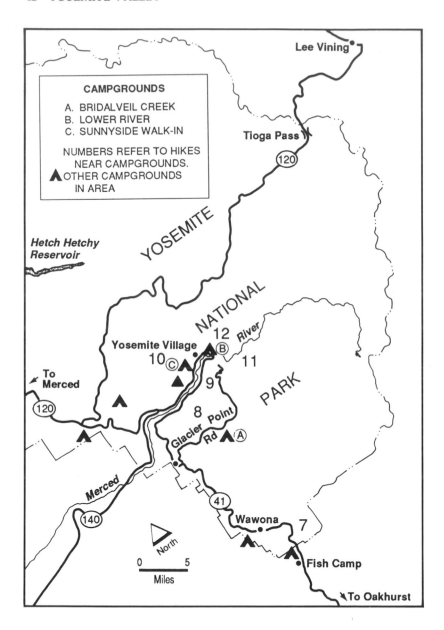

If you want to camp while you're visiting the valley, you'll need to plan ahead. Sunnyside Walk-in Campground is the only option for impromptu camping. Otherwise, make reservations through Ticketron. Campground reservations can be obtained in person at Ticketron offices or by writing to Ticketron Reservations, PO Box 2715, San Francisco, California 94126. Reservations cannot be made more than 8 weeks in advance (but make them as early as possible if you want a spot).

Once in Yosemite Valley, you'll want to stop in at the visitor center in Yosemite Village for maps and trail information. Then make use of the free valley shuttle bus to reach your trailhead. You won't need a permit for day hikes in Yosemite National Park, but there are certain park regulations you should be aware of.

There is an entry fee required of all vehicles entering the park. Dogs are not allowed on unpaved trails in Yosemite, and firearms are not permitted in the park. If you're camping, it's illegal to gather wood (including all dead and down wood) for campfires in Yosemite Valley. This law was enacted in 1989 in an effort to reduce human impact on the valley floor and to lessen the amount of campfire smoke generated by the thousands of campground visitors that stay here every summer night.

Because of ongoing problems with marauding bears in Yosemite National Park, federal law mandates proper storage of food. This means using the bear-proof food lockers that are provided in all Yosemite campgrounds. Irresponsible campers have contributed to the delinquency, deportation, and eventual destruction of countless Yosemite black bears in recent years. Remember, if a bear steals your supper, you're the one that's breaking the law!

If you're planning an overnight visit, or if you want to gather camping or hiking information before you drive into the park, write to Yosemite National Park, PO Box 577, Yosemite, California 95389.

If you'd like to enhance your appreciation of your Yosemite experience, consider doing some background reading on the history of the park (see Further Reading for recommendations).

## CAMPGROUNDS

**Bridalveil Creek Campground** *(Hike 8, McGurk Meadow; Hike 9, Taft Point and Sentinel Dome)* The most wonderful thing about this pleasant campground is that it's open to campers without reservations, a rarity in the always overflowing Yosemite environs. However, you'll want to arrive early in the day if you hope to claim one of the more than 100 sites for tents or motorhomes.

To reach Bridalveil Creek Campground, turn onto Glacier Point Road from the Chinquapin junction on Highway 41 (33.0 miles north of Oakhurst). Drive 8.0 miles up the paved road to reach the campground. With a resident campground host and frequent evening firesides, Bridalveil Creek Campground has much to offer.

Perhaps one of the campground's biggest selling points is its proximity to Glacier Point, the famous Yosemite Valley viewpoint that draws in visitors by the hundreds every summer day. Glacier Point's matchless vista is definitely worth the 16-mile drive up

Glacier Point Road (8.0 miles from Bridalveil Creek Campground), worth the inevitable hunt for a parking spot, and worth the crowds of ice-cream-eating, camera-toting tourists it attracts.

Arrive in the early evening, and linger long enough to watch the sunset paint the mountains pink. Seeing the light fade slowly on the face of Half Dome is an unforgettable experience. Stay another hour and watch the moonrise, too.

Sites at Bridalveil Creek Campground offer fireplaces and picnic tables. There are flush toilets as well. The campground is open June to September. No reservations. Moderate fee.

**Lower River Campground** *(Hike 10, Upper Yosemite Fall; Hike 11, Vernal and Nevada Falls; Hike 12, Mirror Lake)* Sprawled along the Merced River in Yosemite Valley, the vast and always crowded Lower River Campground is a good representative of the valley's handful of reservation campgrounds. You must have advance reservations through Ticketron in order to claim one of the campground's more than 130 sites for tents or motorhomes. And you won't have any solitude or quietness once you get inside. However, you will have convenient access to the treasures of Yosemite Valley, and that should be worth the price.

Lower River Campground is served by Shuttle Stop No. 2. It's a short trip to Yosemite Village and the visitor center from the campground. Sites offer fireplaces, picnic tables, and the ever-present bear boxes. There are flush toilets too. The campground is open May to October. Reservations required. Moderate fee.

**Sunnyside Walk-in Campground** *(Hike 10, Upper Yosemite Fall; Hike 11, Vernal and Nevada Falls; Hike 12, Mirror Lake)* Sunnyside Walk-in Campground is the only nonreservation campground on the Yosemite Valley floor open to visitors with vehicles. Getting a site can be an iffy proposition, as Sunnyside Walk-in Campground is almost always full by evening. Arrive early in the day to claim one of the 38 tentspots.

Sunnyside Walk-in Campground is just west of Yosemite Lodge, between Shuttle Stop Nos. 7 and 8. There's a large parking lot for vehicles, and it's a short walk to campsites. Because of its nature, the campground attracts mainly youthful vacationers and travelers. As such, it's often noisy and always crowded, but it's also an interesting slice of Yosemite life.

Shaded sites offer fireplaces, picnic tables, and obligatory bear boxes for food. There are flush toilets. The campground is open all year. No reservations. Minimal fee.

*Despite its lean, the Grizzly Giant is in fine condition for a 2,700-year-old tree!*

● ● ● ● ● ● ● ● ● ● ● ● ● ● ● ● ● ● ● ● ● ● ● ● ● ●

# 7 MARIPOSA GROVE OF GIANT SEQUOIAS

Distance: 4.7 miles (loop)
Difficulty: Moderate
Starting point: 5,600 feet
High point: 6,700 feet
Map: USGS Yosemite 15′

Despite the hordes of tourists the Mariposa Grove of Giant Sequoias attracts, it is possible to escape the crowds in this stunning grove of ancient trees. Shun the crowded tram ride to the upper grove and take this 4.7-mile hike instead. The exercise will only increase your appreciation for the giants you walk beside.

Access to this hike can be gained from Highway 41, north of Fish Camp and south of Wawona. From Yosemite National Park's south entrance station, drive east 2.1 miles to reach the Mariposa Grove. The parking lot at road's end is especially busy at the noon

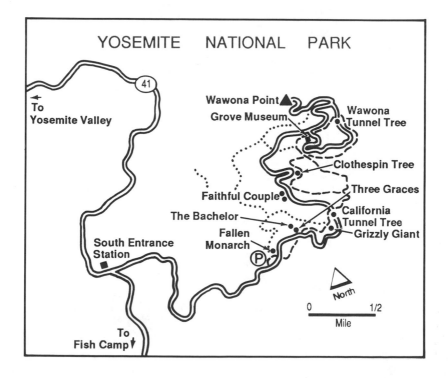

picnic hour, so try to schedule your arrival before or after the midday crunch. Restrooms, drinking fountains, and a gift shop are available to serve the crowds.

Walk to the far end of the parking lot. A signpost and pamphlet/map dispenser mark the start of the trail to the upper grove. Climb gently on a pathway lined by wooden rails to reach the tree called the Fallen Monarch. Its upturned roots are frozen for eternity, looking like the tangled tresses of a toppled giantess.

From the Fallen Monarch, resume walking to reach the Bachelor and Three Graces, pausing at the informational plaques along the way. You'll reach the famous Grizzly Giant at 0.8 mile. The largest tree in the Mariposa Grove, the Grizzly Giant is marked by a decided lean. But that's quite understandable considering its estimated age of 2,700 years.

Continue straight uphill past the Grizzly Giant to get the best angle on its tilt. Return to the Grizzly Giant and descend with the path toward the California Tunnel Tree. The tunnel was cut in 1895 so that stagecoaches could carry awestruck visitors through the tree. You'll lose most of your fellow hikers here as they pause for photos and turn back toward the parking lot.

Climb steadily and steeply from the Tunnel Tree. Pass a turnoff for the Clothespin Tree, and continue uphill to reach the paved tram road and a junction with the Upper Loop Trail at 1.5 miles.

Go right on the Upper Loop Trail, skirting along the hillside beneath a host of sequoias. The trail climbs steadily for a while. At the crest of the climb, watch for the toppled Wawona Tunnel Tree down the hillside to the left. Veer downhill on an unsigned path to reach the tree. The Wawona Tunnel Tree fell in 1969, the victim of record winter snows. Between 1881 and 1969, millions of visitors drove through the tunnel that was hacked through this giant for a labor fee of $75.

From the Wawona Tunnel Tree, walk up the tram road for about 20 yards to gain a trail signed for the Grove Museum. Take the trail downhill to the museum. It offers historical displays and books and, best of all, a drinking fountain.

Continue downhill on the path, passing the restrooms, then regaining the junction with the Upper Loop Trail. Follow signs for the Clothespin Tree. From here, it's 2.0 miles to the parking lot. Descend steadily to reach the Clothespin Tree, transformed into an amazing shape by several fires. Proceed downhill to the two trees called the Faithful Couple.

From the Faithful Couple, go left along the tram road a short distance, then regain the footpath and wind along the hillside to a junction with the trail down to the Grizzly Giant. Go right to retrace your route to the parking lot.

● ● ● ● ● ● ● ● ● ● ● ● ●
# 8  MCGURK MEADOW

Distance: 2.0 miles round trip
Difficulty: Easy
Starting point: 7,200 feet
High point: 7,200 feet
Total climb: 300 feet
Map: USGS Yosemite 15'

This page: *Ranger buttons*
Next page: *Bigelow's sneezeweed*

Bridalveil Creek Campground provides excellent access to this pleasant, level hike to a dazzling wildflower meadow. It's possible to begin right from the campground, but this does add about 2.0 miles to the overall mileage. This is a good excursion for families with little hikers and a nice, easy walk for campers looking for a place to stroll.

To reach the signed trailhead for McGurk Meadow, turn onto Glacier Point Road from the Chinquapin junction on Highway 41 (33.0 miles north of Oakhurst). Drive east on the paved thoroughfare for 7.6 miles (if you reach the turnoff for Bridalveil Creek Campground, you've gone too far). Watch closely for the trailhead sign. There's a small parking pulloff about 100 yards beyond.

Walk north into the forest and reach a sign for Dewey Point (3.9 miles) soon afterward. Descend gently as you begin, then gain level walking through a blighted lodgepole pine forest. Evidence of the destructive work of pine beetles is everywhere.

The way is lined with Brewer's lupine, angelica, and yarrow as you reach another sign for Dewey Point and begin descending gradually. California corn lily and fireweed brighten the forest floor, and the air is sweet with the aroma of a plethora of lupine. Sharp-eyed, quiet hikers may spot mule deer sauntering through the trees.

Pass an old wooden shelter (on the left) as you approach McGurk Meadow. You'll reach a small footbridge across a creek at 0.8 mile. Pause to gaze at the display of wildflowers crouched beside the water. The glowing white faces of yampah glitter in the grass, and bright Bigelow's sneezeweed attracts scores of butterflies.

Cross the bridge, then leave the main trail and angle left along the edge of a stand of trees to explore more of the meadow. (The official trail continues on to Dewey Point.) Try to stay on established paths as much as possible, avoiding the Indian paintbrush, Brewer's lupine, and yellow cinquefoil that weave the meadow's delicate carpet.

You'll find an old footpath cutting through the trees. Arrive at another, larger section of the meadow at 1.0 mile. A lodgepole island in the grass provided shade for grazing cattle in years gone by. If you look closely, you can find evidence of the cows' compacted trails by noting the lines of differing vegetation angling toward the trees.

As you linger in the meadow, you'll spot the blooms of hikers gentian, alpine gentian, yampah, and meadow goldenrod. Watch for the quicksilver shapes of fish in the small creek, savor the sweet scent of grass and sun, then turn home, renewed by the timeless loveliness of this quiet meadow.

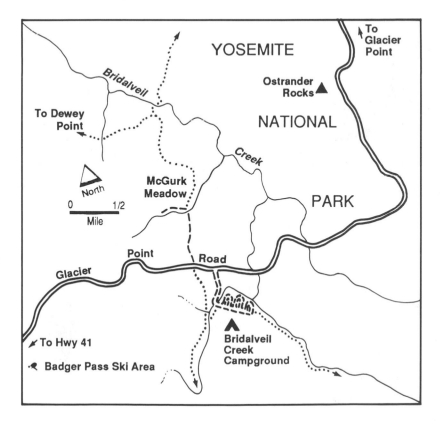

• • • • • • • • • • • • • • • • • • • • • • • • • • •

# 9 TAFT POINT AND SENTINEL DOME

Distance: 5.4 miles (loop)
Difficulty: Moderate
Starting point: 7,880 feet
High point: 8,120 feet
Total climb: 1,280 feet
Map: USGS Yosemite Valley 7.5'

You won't have the usual Yosemite crowds to keep you company on this hike, but it's not because of any lack of scenery—the view from the top of Sentinel Dome is one of Yosemite National Park's finest. Because the trailhead isn't on the valley floor, Sentinel Dome and Taft Point are a little lonelier and, perhaps, a little more appealing than many of the busier Yosemite trails.

*A withered Jeffrey pine frames the spectacular view from Sentinel Dome.*

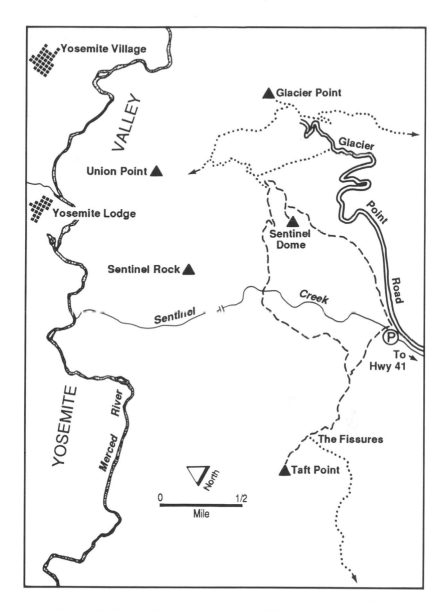

To reach the trailhead for Sentinel Dome, turn onto Glacier Point Road from the Chinquapin junction on Highway 41 (33.0 miles north of Oakhurst). Drive east on the paved thoroughfare for 13.2 miles, and watch for a signed pulloff for Taft Point/Sentinel Dome. It's 2.3 miles before Glacier Point and 5.6 miles beyond Bridalveil Creek Campground.

Leave the parking area and descend slightly to a trail sign

where you'll go left for Taft Point. Set out beneath lodgepole pines and red firs, descending gently to cross a small stream. Brewer's lupine and broadleaf lupine brighten the trailside.

Enjoy level walking to a trail junction at 0.6 mile. Continue straight for The Fissures and Taft Point. Bracken ferns, California corn lily, and small leopard lily line the way. Descend gently and lose the red fir shade as the grade steepens and you approach the edge of a rocky platform at 1.2 miles.

If you have small children along, keep them close here. Admire The Fissures from a respectful distance. These five deep clefts in the rocky cliff face seem to fall forever toward the floor of Yosemite Valley.

Make your way past The Fissures to the rocky knoll known as Taft Point, named in honor of President William Howard Taft's visit to Yosemite Valley in 1909. The view of Yosemite Falls and El Capitan is magnificent, and the valley floor is a stomach-twisting eternity away.

To continue on toward Sentinel Dome, backtrack 0.7 mile to the junction signed for Sentinel Dome. Go left, descending steadily through a forest of Jeffrey pines and red firs. You'll catch glimpses of Sentinel Dome through the trees as you walk. Swing down along the edge of the cliff face, winding through an open area of Indian paintbrush and manzanita.

Cross a creek and begin climbing gently beneath lodgepole pines and red firs. The grade increases as the trail negotiates a series of switchbacks. Reach a trail junction at 3.8 miles, and go right for Sentinel Dome. Continue climbing steeply, cross an unpaved access road, and scramble uphill to gain the summit of Sentinel Dome at 4.3 miles.

You'll be breathing hard by the time you stop, and the view will take away what little breath the climb has left you. Pull up a comfortable boulder and savor one of Yosemite's finest panoramas. Beginning with Mount Hoffmann and working in a clockwise direction, look for Echo Peaks, Clouds Rest, Half Dome, Liberty Cap, Nevada Fall, the Cathedral Range with Mount Lyell, the Clark Range with Mount Clark, Gray Peak, Red Peak, the Yosemite Valley opening, El Capitan, and Yosemite Falls.

If you're a photographer, the gnarled old Jeffrey pine that rules the summit of Sentinel Dome makes a dramatic frame for the distant mountains. And if you're not a photographer, claim a bit of shade beneath the Jeffrey's weathered trunk and simply enjoy the view.

To regain your starting point, retrace your steps down the slope and turn right onto an old asphalt footpath (unsigned). You'll spot a sign for the parking lot soon after. The trail has ducks and "trail" signs to help you find your way across the barren rocks. Even so, it's a little difficult to follow, so be sharp as you descend. Stay with the trail and reach the parking lot at 5.4 miles.

*A hiker pauses at a precipice beside The Fissures.*

• • • • • • • • • • • • • • • • • • • • • • • •

# 10   UPPER YOSEMITE FALL

Distance: 6.8 miles round trip
Difficulty: Strenuous
Starting point: 3,990 feet
High point: 6,720 feet
Total climb: 3,230 feet
Map: USGS Yosemite Valley 7.5'

Like Hike 11, Vernal and Nevada Falls, this hike to Upper Yosemite Fall is extremely challenging, taking in an elevation gain of 2,730 feet with a punishing 135 switchbacks. Begin early in the day to beat the heat, and pack along plenty of liquids to replenish the water you'll perspire and pant away.

Access to the trailhead for Upper Yosemite Fall can be gained from the Sunnyside Walk-in Campground in Yosemite Valley. There's a large parking lot beside the gas station. Walk toward the fall along the west edge of the parking lot, and reach a sign for Upper Yosemite Fall soon after.

Begin climbing steeply in several short switchbacks between canyon live oaks, bay trees, and manzanita. The trail is sandy, and there are several sections of fitted stones that can be very slick, especially when descending. After about 30 minutes of climbing, you'll begin enjoying views down into Yosemite Valley.

Reach a rail-guarded viewpoint, offering a spectacular vista of Half Dome, Mount Clark, and the Clark Range. You'll have a bird's-eye view of Yosemite Lodge and the Sunnyside Walk-in Campground, too. Resume climbing steeply through a few sandy switchbacks, then begin a descent as you skirt along the steep hillside.

The descent is welcome, but unwelcome; more climbing is ahead. Get your first good look at Upper Yosemite Fall in this section, framed by the branches of canyon live oak. If the climb is taking more of a toll than you anticipated, this is a good stopping point. There's a long, tough haul ahead.

Continue descending in the shade of Jeffrey pines, black oaks, and incense cedars. The danger of rockslides is very real on this trail. Previous slides are evident as you walk. The descent ends and the climb resumes as a rocky path leads up a narrow canyon.

Views of the Clark Range broaden as you gain altitude. The climb is long and gruesome, so pause to admire the scenery. You can study the trailside wildflowers, too. Scarlet penstemon blazes among the rocks, and the blossoms of blue elderberry are thick on hillside bushes.

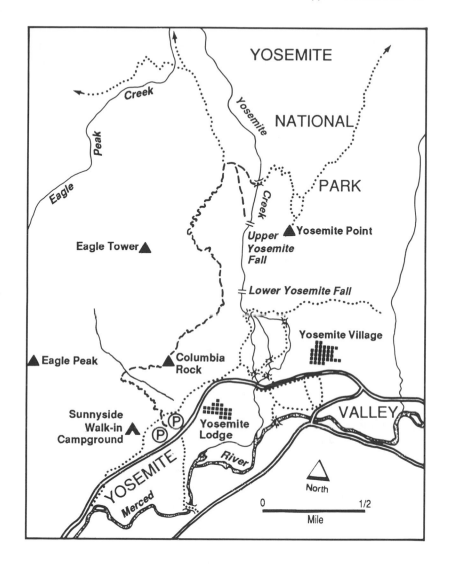

Plod steadily uphill for just short of an eternity. You'll be thankful for an early start as you cross this open, shadeless section. And you'll be even more thankful when you reach the top at last.

Savor the coolness of the shaded glen on the ridgetop, and follow trail signs for Yosemite Falls. There's a short overlook trail that takes off to the right as the trail branches. The overlook is worth a trip, but be careful on the cliff face. The overlook offers a half view of Half Dome and a stomach-twisting look down on Yosemite Valley, as well as a unique angle on Yosemite Creek's dive to Lower Yosemite Fall.

Return to the main trail and continue to the banks of Yosemite Creek. There's a wooden footbridge crossing here, and an additional 0.8-mile climb leads on to Yosemite Point and another awesome view, if you've got the energy.

Otherwise, linger on the edge of the swift-flowing waterway, munch your lunch and cool your toes. The water is tempting, and you'll surely see some swimmers, but think about the dizzying drop you just peered over, and be cautious.

## • • • • • • • • • • •
## 11 VERNAL AND NEVADA FALLS

Distance: 5.9 miles (loop)
Difficulty: Strenuous
Starting point: 4,020 feet
High point: 6,000 feet
Map: USGS Yosemite Valley 7.5'

*A panhandling ground squirrel*

This challenging hike offers a stiff climb and an abundance of spectacular scenery. The trail is rough and dangerous in spots, so don't bring along small children. Do bring a lunch, a lot of liquids, and a good supply of film, as you'll want to make this an all-day, leisurely excursion.

Reach the trailhead by taking the Yosemite Valley park shuttle to Stop No. 16, Happy Isles. Drinking water and toilets are available at the stop. Start out on a paved pathway, and cross the Merced River on a sturdy bridge. You'll reach a sign for the High Sierra Loop Trail, and begin climbing steadily on the paved trail beside the water.

This spot also marks the start of the 212-mile John Muir Trail, a Sierra gem that winds its way southward to the summit of Mount Whitney, the highest peak in the Continental United States. Except for a brief side trip on the scenic Mist Trail, the entire hike follows the John Muir Trail.

Bay trees make the moist air fragrant, and canyon live oak is everywhere. Descend briefly to another bridge where there is a view of Vernal Fall. This is your last chance for restrooms and drinking water.

Climb beside the tumultuous Merced in the shade of bigleaf maples, Douglas firs, and incense cedars. Arrive at another junction and stay beside the water, following the sign for Vernal Fall via the Mist Trail. Watch for a streamside view of the fall soon afterward. If you've attempted to beat the crowds with an early start, you may miss the magic of the sunlight on the water—the sun's rays don't reach this shaded spot until almost 10 A.M.

Continue climbing toward the mist-shrouded gorge, and arrive at a long set of stairs, hewn in the solid rock. Walk carefully, as the heavy mist makes the stones very slick. The high steps and the incline will have you puffing, so pause to catch your breath and savor the scenery as often as you feel the need.

Early in the summer, wildflowers are abundant in the lushness of the gorge. And rainbows arc across the water, painted by the blended talents of sun and moisture. Continue climbing and regain the dirt trail beneath the trees, bidding a reluctant farewell to the refreshing mist.

Another set of stairs (and a welcome railing) will take you steeply up to the top of Vernal Fall. There's a fine view down the canyon from the top, and Liberty Cap and Half Dome loom grandly just above. Please obey the signs and stay back from the edge. Both Vernal Fall and Nevada Fall have claimed their share of incautious victims over the years.

Continue upstream past Emerald Pool and a lovely slide of rock and water aptly named the Silver Apron. Again, please remember that these tempting spots in the river are as dangerous as they are beautiful. The trail is rather obscure through here. Look for small brown "trail" signs as you walk.

Reach a junction signed for the John Muir Trail (right) at 1.5 miles. Continue straight for Nevada Fall instead. You'll have great views of Half Dome as you climb. Cross the Merced soon after the junction. Climb through manzanita, then enjoy a welcome stretch of level hiking beneath shade-dropping incense cedars.

Resume climbing on a rocky, shaded path that can be difficult

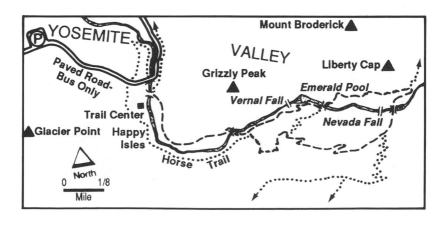

*The unforgettable view of Nevada Fall from the John Muir Trail*

to follow. Ascend a steep, narrow canyon on the left side of the fall, and rejoin the John Muir Trail at another junction when you're at the top. Go right with the trail toward Nevada Fall, breathing your thanks that the climb is over.

The trail will take you back to the Merced River, this time just above its suicidal leap toward the valley far below. You can descend to a rail-guarded viewpoint before you reach the river, then walk back to the sun-warmed stones along the river's edge to enjoy a picnic lunch and rest your weary legs.

Sierra junipers and ponderosa pines offer bits of shade, and beggar squirrels will do their best to steal your lunch if you try to close your eyes more than a moment. The water is tempting, but be very careful if you decide to douse your toes.

To begin your return trip to the valley floor, continue with the John Muir Trail, crossing the Merced River, then descending along an open cliff face, with fantastic views of Half Dome and Liberty Cap.

Pass the junction signed for Vernal Fall and the Mist Trail, and continue down on the John Muir Trail, descending steadily through a seemingly endless succession of switchbacks. Old, worn asphalt and loose, rounded gravel make for a slippery combination, so watch your step.

Reach a junction with a horse trail and continue straight on the foot trail. You'll arrive at another junction immediately afterward. Go left here to join the trail you ascended on.

• • • • • • • • • • • • • • • • • • • • • • • • •

# 12 MIRROR LAKE

Distance: 4.7 miles (loop)
Difficulty: Easy
Starting point: 4,000 feet
High point: 4,150 feet
Map: USGS Yosemite Valley 7.5'

The walk to Mirror Lake is the most popular short hike in Yosemite National Park. As such, it's incredibly crowded on almost every summer day. Even so, it's a pleasant, easy jaunt, providing a "picture-perfect" look at Mount Watkins and Half Dome, reflected in Yosemite's most famous "mirror." Add in a loop along Tenaya Creek to lose some of the people and gain a rare slice of Yosemite solitude.

Access to the the trailhead is from Yosemite Valley Shuttle

*Shrinking Mirror Lake is a reflection of its former self.*

Stop No. 17. The bus once ran right to Mirror Lake, but the route was changed to cut down on the impact of the hordes (a bit). Set out on a paved road and walk toward the Tenaya Creek Bridge.

Just before the bridge, veer right to gain a dirt bridle trail along the creek. The vast majority of Mirror Lake's visitors will follow the asphalt route to reach the lake, although the trail is much more pleasant, even with the occasional horse droppings. Traffic is fairly light on the bridle trail. Just step off the path when the guided horse caravans come through.

Walk in comparative solitude beneath canyon live oaks, Douglas firs, white firs, and incense cedars. Pacific dogwoods brighten the forest with their creamy white bracts in spring, and bigleaf maples and California bays add to the variety of trees.

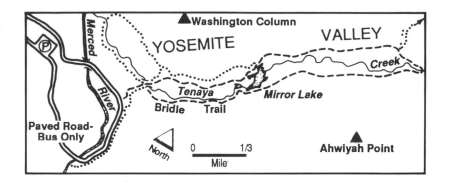

The chortle of Tenaya Creek will keep you company as you continue (and you can watch the hordes of people pound the asphalt pathway on the other side). Ascend gently to a small wooden footbridge. You can shorten your walk considerably by crossing here and taking the asphalt to Mirror Lake. To continue on the pleasant route, stay with the bridle trail, passing a popular swimming hole soon after.

Walk on and reach the edge of shallow Mirror Lake. The "lake" is little more than a gradually shrinking pond, as each year the silt gathers to make Mirror Lake a little smaller. Wander down onto the path across the meadow to gain a "reflective" look at Half Dome and Mount Watkins across the water.

Turn back toward the bridle trail, and continue through a cool, dark forest of massive incense cedars. Ferns are thick beneath the trees, and the terrain is mostly level. Reach a wooden bridge across Tenaya Creek at 2.3 miles. The creek is clear and inviting, with many shallow pools for trailworn toes.

Cross the bridge and turn back toward Mirror Lake. Reach a junction with the Tenaya Lake Trail at 2.6 miles. Continue straight for Mirror Lake, and enjoy level, quiet walking through the forest for another mile. You'll spot the glitter of Mirror Lake's surface through the trees at the 3.6-mile point.

Keep left when the trail branches, and reach the asphalt road again. You may want to wander back down to the edge of the lake for a final look at Tenaya Gorge, ruled by Half Dome and Mount Watkins. Return to the asphalt and cruise back to the shuttle stop with the crowds on foot and bicycles.

# CHAPTER THREE

• • • • • • • • •

# Tioga Pass (Highway 120)

At 9,945 feet, Tioga Pass is the highest autoroute across the Sierra Nevada Mountains. The Tioga Pass Summit marks the eastern boundary of Yosemite National Park, and the road provides access to some of the Sierra's most spectacular scenery. Although it's not besieged with the tremendous hordes that threaten to overwhelm Yosemite Valley, the Tioga Pass area of Yosemite National Park is far from lonely. Resign yourself to a lot of company on the trails.

The present-day Highway 120 follows the general route of the old Tioga Road. This wagon road was constructed to provide a transport route for the anticipated flow of supplies and ore to and from mining settlements such as Bennettville, on the park's eastern border (see Hike 19). The predecessor of the old Tioga Road was the Mono Indian trail across Mono Pass.

In addition to the wealth of Sierra Nevada history, a drive along Highway 120 entails a wealth of scenery. Be sure to avail yourself of the many roadside pulloffs, where views and informational plaques abound. The Tuolumne Meadows Information Center (8.0 miles southwest of the Tioga Pass Summit) is a great place to pick up maps, literature, current trail information, and camping recommendations.

You won't need a permit for day hikes off Tioga Pass. If you're planning an overnight visit, or if you want to gather camping or hiking information before you drive into the park, write to Yosemite National Park, PO Box 577, Yosemite, California 95389.

Camping options on Tioga Pass are varied, ranging from reservation facilities to walk-in sites to primitive campgrounds slightly off the beaten track. If everything is full the day you visit, check out the campgrounds listed in chapter 4 as other possibilities. As in Yosemite Valley, hungry black bears are a continual problem on Tioga Pass. Proper food storage is essential to your camping happiness. Use bear boxes when provided, don't leave food on picnic tables or in tents, and cover all food and coolers stowed in your car.

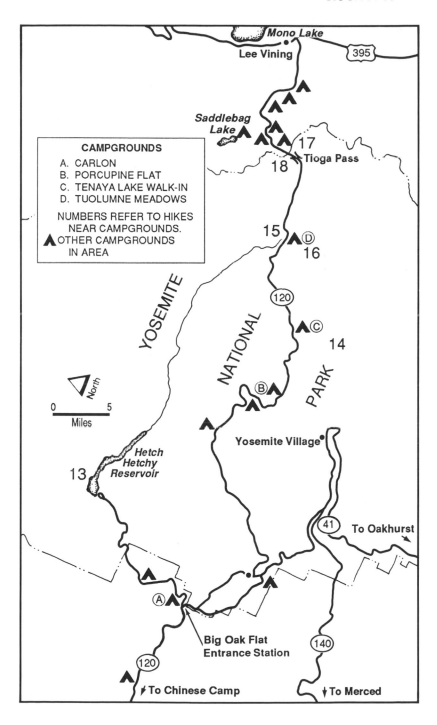

# CAMPGROUNDS

**Carlon Campground** *(Hike 13, Hetch Hetchy and Rancheria Falls)*   A super option for the reservationless Yosemite camper, rustic Carlon Campground is situated just a mile off Highway 120 as you approach Yosemite National Park from the west. To find the campground, follow signs for Hetch Hetchy Reservoir from the Hetch Hetchy junction, 1.1 miles west of the Big Oak Flat Entrance Station, and drive 1.0 mile to reach the site.

This free campground's 16 or so tentspots are usually full (and often noisy!) on weekends, so come early if you want a spot. There's water available from a hand-pumped well; however, toilets are of the non-flush variety. Even so, this is a pleasant, shaded spot, with walk-in sites right on the South Fork of the Tuolumne River. Open May to November. No reservations. No fee.

**Porcupine Flat Campground** *(Hike 14, Clouds Rest)*   You can reach Porcupine Flat Campground from the Tioga Pass Road, 9.2 miles east of the White Wolf road junction. This undeveloped campground is a good option for the spur-of-the-moment Yosemite camper, as reservations are not accepted and sites are often available until early afternoon.

The most pleasant of the campground's 55 sites are in the rear of the campground, where a small creek and a grassy meadow attract grazing deer. The road into the campground is rough and unpaved, however. Those with motorhomes won't want to venture in too far.

Campsites offer fireplaces, picnic tables, and non-flush toilets. Be very careful with foodstuffs, as bears are frequent visitors. There is no drinking water at the campground. Open June to October. No reservations. Moderate fee.

**Tenaya Lake Walk-in Campground** *(Hike 14, Clouds Rest)*   This exceedingly busy campground boasts 50 tentsites along the shoreline of lovely Tenaya Lake. Come early in the day for your best chance at an empty spot. Cars can be left in the large lot adjacent to the campground, and it's a short walk to the sites from there.

The trailhead for Hike 14, Clouds Rest, is right at the campground, and sites offer fireplaces and picnic tables. Flush toilets and drinking water are available, as well. Open June to October. No reservations. Moderate fee.

**Tuolumne Meadows Campground** *(Hike 15, Tuolumne Meadows Walk; Hike 16, Elizabeth Lake; Hike 17, Mount Dana; Hike 18, Gaylor Lakes)*   This sprawling campground is a particularly nice base for Hike 16, Elizabeth Lake, as the trailhead is right in the campground.

*Two hikers savor the view of mighty Kolana Rock from a perch above Rancheria Falls.*

Reach the signed Tuolumne Meadows Campground by driving a short distance east of the Tuolumne Meadows Information Center on the Tioga Pass Road.

Check out the unique mound of granite known as Pothole Dome while you're staying at Tuolumne Meadows Campground. The short but steep scramble to the dome's summit yields a wonderful view down onto Tuolumne Meadows and east to Lembert Dome and Mount Dana.

Pothole Dome is 1.5 miles west of the Tuolumne Meadows Information Center, on the north side of Highway 120. There's a busy parking pulloff here. Pothole Dome's famous "potholes" were formed by flowing water trapped beneath a passing glacier. Like marble-lined bathtubs, the holes offer comfortable spots to plunk yourself down and enjoy the scenery, but please be sure to watch your step on the polished granite.

Half of the more than 300 campsites at Tuolumne Meadows Campground are available on a first-come, first-serve basis (no reservations), and half can be reserved through Ticketron. Sites are available for both tents and motorhomes. Arrive very early in the day if you hope to claim a nonreservation spot. There are a limited number of walk-in sites available as well.

Campsites offer fireplaces and picnic tables, and the campground has flush toilets and drinking water. Open June to October. Fees vary.

• • • • • • • • • • • • • • • • • • • • • • • • • • •

## 13   HETCH HETCHY AND RANCHERIA FALLS

Distance: 13.0 miles round trip
Difficulty: Strenuous
Starting point: 3,810 feet
High point: 4,720 feet
Total climb: 1,460 feet
Maps: USGS Hetch Hetchy Reservoir 15' and USGS Lake Eleanor 15'

This hike along the shore of Hetch Hetchy Reservoir, culminating at Rancheria Falls, is a wonderful early-season destination for those "just itching" to begin their summer hiking with a Sierra jaunt. As the months go by, the heat increases and the attractions of this low-elevation walk begin to fade. However, an early morning start and a long midafternoon picnic at the falls can make this hike pleasant on almost any summer day.

Be wary of three Hetch Hetchy dangers on this walk. Rattlesnakes are present in these lower elevations, so keep an eye out as you hike. Bears are abundant in the region, especially in the back-packer camping area near Rancheria Falls. If you're alert and use common sense, you shouldn't have any problems. Poison oak is thick along portions of the trail. Know what it looks like (see photo-graph), and do your best to avoid contact.

To reach the trailhead for Rancheria Falls, turn off Highway 120 1.1 miles west of the Big Oak Flat Entrance Station on the west side of Yosemite National Park, following signs for Hetch Hetchy Reservoir. Drive the paved Evergreen Road, then the Hetch Hetchy Road, and arrive at the reservoir after 16.0 miles. You'll pass a Yosemite National Park entrance station on the way. There is a national park entrance fee required of all vehicles approaching Hetch Hetchy Reservoir.

There's a paved lot and abundant roadside parking beside O'Shaughnessy Dam, where the trail begins. Depending on the time of day and day of the week you visit, you may have to park quite a distance from the trailhead. This trail is extremely popular with backpackers, and weekend crowds are big.

Start out across O'Shaughnessy Dam, named for the engineer who headed the Hetch Hetchy Reservoir project that began in 1914 and culminated in the creation of this 8-mile-long reservoir, which provides drinking water for the city of San Francisco. There is a drinking fountain half way across the dam, if you need to fill a couple of water bottles.

Pause on the dam and gaze up the canyon, envisioning the grandeur of this rugged valley before it was "tamed" into a reser-voir. The view is of Hetch Hetchy Dome and Wapama Falls on the north side of the canyon, and the sheer face of Kolana Rock on the south. Continue across the dam and through a 500-foot-long tunnel, then follow an old roadbed to a trail sign at 0.3 mile.

Hike along the level roadbed just above the reservoir, with

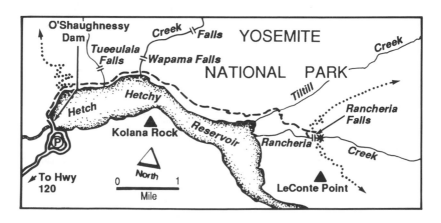

digger pines, California bay trees, manzanita, and canyon live oak for company. Begin a gentle ascent and keep a sharp eye out for poison oak as you continue.

The flowers are gorgeous here in early season. Look for brightly colored farewell-to-spring and lovely purple elegant brodiaea as you walk.

Reach a junction at 1.0 mile and go right for Rancheria Creek. Here, the mostly level trail abandons the roadbed and leads through a flower-covered wonderland of brodiaea, farewell-to-spring, yampah, and mariposa lily. Arrive at seasonal Tueeulala Falls at 1.5 miles. There's not much to see if the water's scarce, but it's a lovely veil of lace and stone when the flow is heavy.

Continue on with the rocky trail and gain sight of Wapama Falls at 1.9 miles. The cool cascades are particularly alluring on a hot summer day, especially because the reservoir itself is closed to swimming. Across the reservoir, the sheer cliff face of Kolana Rock looks as though a knife had swept down in a single blow, slicing the stone from sky to water.

Arrive at Wapama Falls at 2.4 miles. A long stream of water pours over the canyon lip far overhead, then descends in great leaps, tumbling over massive boulders. The cool mist of the falls is invigorating as you cross the water on a series of steel-frame bridges.

Proceed into a forested swathe of California bay, oak, and poison oak as you begin to climb away from the reservoir at a steady pace. There is a nice view back to Wapama Falls at 3.3 miles. Enjoy a brief descent at the 4.1-mile mark, then follow a level trail along a hillside that's gorgeous with elegant brodiaea.

Cross a noisy stream on a footbridge at 5.2 miles, then climb steadily to get your first peek at Rancheria Creek 0.5 mile later. If you're in the mood for a little frolicking, the temptation of the pools and water slides here might provoke a detour. Otherwise, continue up with the trail as you follow the path of Rancheria Creek.

The unmarked trail branching off to the right at 6.0 miles leads to a shaded camping area along the creek (renowned for its proliferation of hungry bears) and to one of the best views up the canyon to Rancheria Falls. Stay with the main trail to arrive at a signed junction at 6.4 miles, and go straight for Pleasant Valley.

A bridge spans Rancheria Creek just above the falls at 6.5 miles. The view is wonderful from here. Gaze down the creek canyon and admire Rancheria Falls frothing just below, then follow the ribbon of Rancheria Creek out to Hetch Hetchy Reservoir and magnificent Kolana Rock.

Although you probably won't want to do your creekside toe wiggling here, you can savor a leisurely picnic with a view, then begin your long backtrack to the parking area (with perhaps a few stops for splashing in the creek's cool waters along the way).

*Amazing formations of exfoliated granite grace the climb to Clouds Rest.*

## 14   CLOUDS REST

Distance: 14.0 miles round trip
Difficulty: Strenuous
Starting point: 8,150 feet
High point: 9,930 feet
Total climb: 2,280 feet
Map: USGS Tuolumne Meadows 15'

This day hike to the aptly named Clouds Rest is not an outing for the timid or the out of shape. It's a tough hike, but an exhilarating one. And you'll be rewarded with a matchless vista of Half Dome and its Yosemite surroundings.

One warning—this is not a hike to attempt when thunderclouds are threatening. Clouds Rest is an exposed, lofty patch of granite, and it's definitely not the place to be when there's a chance of lightning. Your best bet is to start very early in the day, to reach your goal before Yosemite's customary afternoon thunderclouds begin to gather.

To reach the trailhead for Clouds Rest, turn off Tioga Pass Road at the Tenaya Lake Walk-in Campground (at the west end of Tenaya Lake), and leave your car in the large parking lot. The trailhead sign on the road says "Sunrise" (for the Sunrise Lakes). Follow the signs for the Sunrise High Sierra Camp (HSC) as you begin your hike.

Cross an outlet stream from Tenaya Lake, then wind through a meadow/forest setting on a level trail. California corn lily, broadleaf lupine, and lodgepole pines thrive beside the path. Cross a second stream and begin climbing gently in the shade of scrappy mountain hemlocks.

The grade increases after 1.5 miles and ascends a rocky slope dotted with broadleaf lupine and Lemmon's paintbrush. The dedicated effort of trail maintenance workers is evident in a pathway painstakingly paved with long-wearing stones.

The ascent becomes more punishing as the trail approaches the summit of the ridge. You'll pick up a whisper of traffic noise from the Tioga Pass Road, visible far below. Breathe a sigh of gratitude (if you have a breath to spare) as you gain the ridgeline and a sign for Clouds Rest (4.7 miles). To the left, a short, level jaunt leads to the Sunrise Lakes, where swimming opportunities abound.

Press on toward Clouds Rest instead, descending steeply for 0.5 mile. Then wind across an alpine meadow lush with broadleaf lupine, Lemmon's paintbrush, and California corn lily. The trail is mostly level as you pass a patch of quaking aspens and a lot of chinquapin.

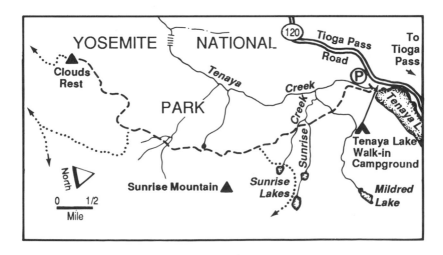

*An exposed ridge leads to the airy summit of Clouds Rest.*

Walk beside a small lake, cross a stream, and begin climbing steadily to another junction signed for Clouds Rest (2.5 miles). Angle right and continue climbing, then enjoy more mellow walking as you wind along the ridgeline leading toward Clouds Rest.

The final ascent to the summit is a steep and somewhat unnerving passage up a narrow ridge composed of piled sheets of granite, reminiscent of a line of toppled dominoes. This last part of the climb can be frightening because of the dropoffs on either side of the ridge, but the footing is good and a careful hiker should have no difficulty conquering the summit.

Once on top, you'll know your heaving lungs and butterfly-filled stomach were small investments for the rewards Clouds Rest has to offer. Half Dome appears to be only an airy leap away, temptingly near across a deep green chasm. And with a little squinting, you'll be able to make out the famous cable trail to the summit of the dome.

Tear your eyes away from Half Dome, and Clouds Rest offers

other treasures. The rich Yosemite Valley lies at your feet in one direction, Tioga Pass Road snakes through granite domes and mounded hills in the other. And a host of Yosemite peaks completes the awesome view. Pull up a flat rock, pull off your shoes and socks, pull out a sandwich, and enjoy the bounty of Clouds Rest.

One reminder—it's easy to lose track of time in such a lovely spot. So keep an eye on your watch, and don't forget the 7-mile descent.

# 15 TUOLUMNE MEADOWS WALK

Distance: 1.0 mile round trip
Difficulty: Easy
Starting point: 8,600 feet
High point: 8,600 feet
Map: USGS Tuolumne Meadows 15'

Here is an easy stroll to fill a spare hour or to help you stretch your legs after a long stint in the car. It's a meadow ramble rich in wildflowers and Yosemite history.

To reach the starting point, turn off Tioga Pass Road just east of the Tuolumne Meadows Information Center at a sign for Lembert Dome/Dog Lake/Soda Springs. Once off Tioga Pass Road, follow the road sign for the "Stables," and park along the shoulder where the road veers right. There is a blocked-off road straight ahead with a trailhead sign for Soda Springs/Parsons Lodge/Glen Aulin.

Circumvent the barrier and walk along the abandoned road as you head out into Tuolumne Meadows. The road follows the course of the Tuolumne River and leads toward the historic Parsons Lodge. The self-guiding trail traces the route of the old Tioga Road, constructed in 1883. Informational plaques along the way point out nearby peaks as well as meadow trees and animals.

Early in the season, enjoy Indian paintbrush, shooting stars, and a variety of other wildflowers. When you pause for a picnic lunch, guard your sandwiches from marauding Belding ground squirrels, accustomed to cashing in on careless tourists.

Reach a junction and keep left to take the lower route along the water. If you go left at the next junction (signed for the visitor center), you can walk down to a bridge across the Tuolumne River, the waterway that nurtures this lush meadow. Retrace your steps to the junction and go left to resume your trek toward Soda Springs and Parsons Lodge.

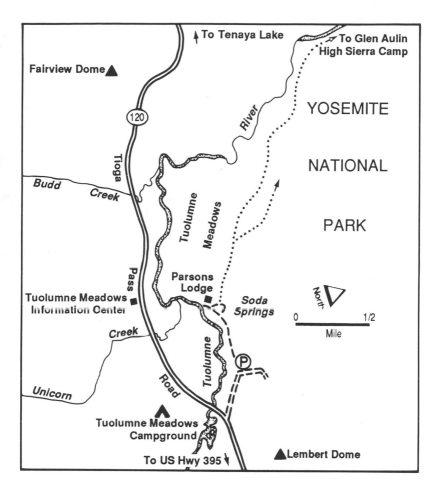

Go right soon after to climb a gentle incline toward the lodge, a handsome stone building surrounded by lodgepole pines. Built in 1915, Parsons Lodge is named for Edward Parsons, past director of the Sierra Club. Be sure to duck inside the building, as the lodge exhibits tell a fascinating tale of the history of Tuolumne Meadows. Postcards and books are available too, and there's a play area where children can sit and draw.

As you turn back toward the starting point, take the upper trail past Soda Springs, a somewhat mucky spring of carbonated water that still bubbles from the ground. John Baptiste Lembert homesteaded 160 acres around Soda Springs in 1885, and in 1901, the fledgling Sierra Club began their annual outings from the site.

Continue past Soda Springs, with views of Lembert Dome straight ahead. Rejoin the old Tioga Road to regain the starting point.

*Afternoon thunderclouds threaten the serenity of Tuolumne Meadows.*

If this short walk simply whets your appetite for more meadow rambling, it's possible to continue west from Parsons Lodge to the Glen Aulin High Sierra Camp, an 11.4-mile round trip. Or you might consider making the scramble up nearby Lembert Dome, an extremely popular meadow-area hike.

• • • • • • • • • • • • • • • • • • • • • • • • • •

# 16  ELIZABETH LAKE

Distance: 4.6 miles round trip
Difficulty: Easy
Starting point: 8,600 feet
High point: 9,580 feet
Map: USGS Tuolumne Meadows 15'

This is a perfect hike for families staying at Tuolumne Meadows Campground, as the trailhead is right at the campground. Or, if you're traveling through on Tioga Pass Road and in the mood for an easy walk to a scenic picnic/swimming spot, Elizabeth Lake is a destination that's hard to beat.

Reach the trailhead for Elizabeth Lake by driving east of the Tuolumne Meadows Information Center, and turn into Tuolumne Meadows Campground. Pause at the manned ranger booth just inside the entrance to request a car parking pass and directions to the trailhead. Take the second left past the booth (a sign at the junction says "Elizabeth Lake Trailhead"), drive through the group camping area, and park beside the restrooms.

The trailhead is just beyond the restroom building. Like the hike to Gaylor Lakes (Hike 18), this walk has been closed to overnight visitors in an effort to preserve the delicate shoreline of Elizabeth Lake.

Begin with a gentle ascent to a junction at 0.1 mile, then continue straight for Elizabeth Lake. Climb steadily for 1.5 miles, walking through a quiet landscape of mountain hemlocks and lodgepole pines. The terrain levels as you walk beside the chortling waterway known as Unicorn Creek.

Emerge into an open meadow and drink in an impressive view

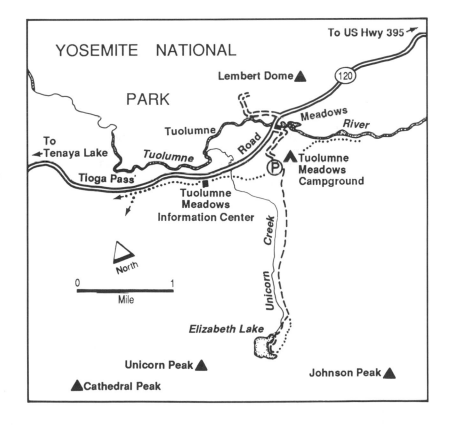

of the white granite cliffs that form the backdrop to Elizabeth Lake. To the right, the distinctive outline of Unicorn Peak gores passing clouds with its pointed summit. Reach another junction and keep to the right along the creek.

If you can tear your eyes away from the scenery ahead, you'll find an awesome panorama behind you as well. Mount Conness and Ragged Peak rule the meadow with their bulky silhouettes. Take your gaze from the skyline and discover a masterpiece at your feet. The meadow is alive with bistort and Indian paintbrush, and the creek dances with colorful stones and darting fish.

Arrive at the shore of Elizabeth Lake and settle in for an afternoon of picnicking and splashing. Shoreside pathways lead in both directions, offering opportunities to seek a bit of solitude or simply soak in the luxuries that Elizabeth Lake has to offer.

## 17  MOUNT DANA

Distance: 5.8 miles round trip
Difficulty: Strenuous
Starting point: 9,950 feet
High point: 13,050 feet
Maps: USGS Tuolumne Meadows 15' and USGS Mono Craters 15'

This hike to the top of Mount Dana is not for everyone. It's a grueling 3,100-foot climb with uphill grades that will have you gasping. But if you don't mind a bit of hard hiking and the prospect of tired muscles at day's end, you'll probably leap at this opportunity to ascend to the summit of the second highest peak in Yosemite National Park. And where else but on Tioga Pass can you climb a 13,050-foot mountain in a single afternoon?

Plan this hike for late summer or early fall to be sure that Mount Dana will be clear of snow, and start as early in the day as possible to beat the heat, the crowds, and, if you're fortunate, the frequent Yosemite thundershowers. If, by chance, a bit of thunder and lightning does brew up before you're finished, head for lower ground immediately. The exposed summit of Mount Dana is no place to linger in an electrical storm.

Reach the trailhead for Mount Dana by driving to the eastside Yosemite entry station on Tioga Pass Road. Parking is available just west of the station, on the north side of the road. This is also the trailhead parking for Gaylor Lakes (Hike 18). There are restrooms at the lot.

*The blossoms of California corn lily enhance the beauty of Mount Dana's lower reaches.*

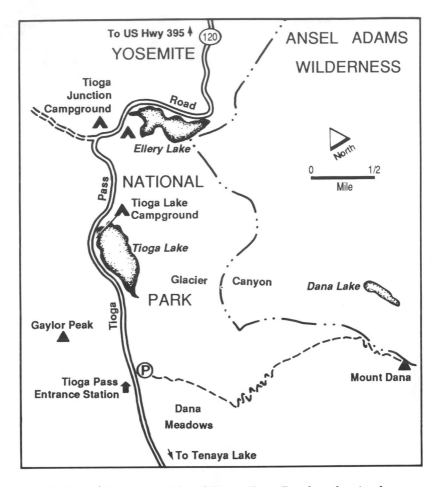

Walk to the south side of Tioga Pass Road and gain the un-signed trail for Mount Dana's summit, beginning your walk with a gentle ascent through the wildflower-packed Dana Meadows. Broadleaf lupine is rampant beneath whitebark and lodgepole pines as the trail climbs past two ponds.

The grade increases markedly as you wind along a rocky hill-side that's an avalanche of Indian paintbrush, cow parsnip, and alpine goldenrod in July. Tumbling creekbeds overflow with yellow monkeyflowers and fragrant swamp onions, making the climb scenic, if strenuous.

Continue up as the ascent becomes more challenging and the wildflowers yet more numerous. Bistort, California corn lily, Coville's columbine, spreading phlox, and cinquefoil compete for every inch of open ground. A score of short switchbacks will take you up and up and up.

Exchange the wildflowers for a more rocky, barren landscape at about 11,000 feet. The footing is quite good, despite the sandy, boulder-strewn terrain, but keep an eye out for the orange paint that marks the sometimes obscure route up the slope. You'll feel the effects of the high elevation as your lungs begin to scream for air. Rest frequently, pausing to enjoy the widening panorama at your feet.

Reach the 11,500-foot level when you arrive at a broad, gently sloping plateau ruled by a large rock cairn. The views are fantastic in all directions, except where the bulk of Mount Dana looms above to the southeast. This is a good spot to stop for a nibble and a break, as a lot of tough climbing is still ahead.

Resume the ascent by angling left (east) on a fairly well-defined trail. Reach a rocky ridgeline and turn upward with it, enjoying impressive views of Dana Lake below and Mono Lake in the hazy distance to the northeast. Watch for the perky blue blossoms of the altitude-loving sky pilot as you climb.

Continue up and up on the ill-defined trail. Just keep heading up the hill, and you shouldn't have any trouble finding your goal. Once on the summit of Mount Dana, enjoy an awesome 360-degree view of Sierra scenery. Break out your sandwiches and a map, and settle in to get your bearings and catch your breath.

• • • • • • • • • • • • • • • • • • • • • • • • •

# 18 GAYLOR LAKES

Distance: 4.0 miles round trip
Difficulty: Moderate
Starting point: 9,950 feet
High point: 10,750 feet
Total climb: 1,200 feet
Map: USGS Tuolumne Meadows 15'

Mile for mile and foot for foot, this hike into the Gaylor Lakes basin offers some of the most scenic hiking for distance and elevation gain found anywhere in the Sierra Nevada. After an initial steep ascent, walking is easy and enjoyable, and children will love the wildflower-lined shores of the Gaylor Lakes. Bring a picnic, a lot of film, and a swimming suit (if you're hearty), and plan to linger all afternoon.

Reach the trailhead for Gaylor Lakes by driving to the eastside Yosemite entry station on Tioga Pass Road. Parking is available just west of the station, on the north side of the road. This is also the trailhead parking for Mount Dana (Hike 17). There are restrooms at the lot.

The hike to Gaylor Lakes is off limits to horses and overnight campers because of the delicate alpine landscape the trail traverses. This helps cut down on the crowds and makes Gaylor Lakes an even more wonderful destination for one-day visitors.

Begin on the path that leaves from the parking lot, climbing steeply on a switchback-studded trail. The hillside is colorful with broadleaf lupine and California corn lily in July and August, and the ascent brings views to the south of Dana Meadows and Mount Dana. Pause for breathers in the shade of the stunted lodgepole pines that cling to the rocky slope.

After about 0.8 mile, reach the ridgetop and gain a view down onto the twin gems that make up Gaylor Lakes. To the west, Unicorn and Cathedral peaks poke through the Yosemite skyline, and Gaylor Peak rules the skyline to the east.

Abandon the ridgetop for the steep descent to Middle Gaylor Lake, winding through scattered whitebark pines and a plethora of wildflowers as you scramble down the hill. Arrive at Middle Gaylor Lake at the 1.0-mile point.

This deep blue beauty is a shimmering saucer of liquid, rimmed by a semicircle of jagged peaks. Stand on the shoreline of Middle Gaylor Lake and gaze across the water, and you'll find yourself wondering what keeps this lovely lake from spilling out.

Angle right around the shore on a well-defined path, then follow the pathway onward through the meadow, ascending gently toward Upper Gaylor Lake. Walk beside a whispering waterway, and pause often to listen to the tales it tells with banks awash in Lemmon's paintbrush, miniature lupine, bistort, and charming little elephant heads.

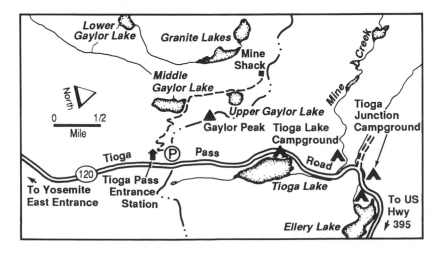

*Snow-flecked Gaylor Peak provides a stunning backdrop to Upper Gaylor Lake.*

Arrive at Upper Gaylor Lake after an unforgettable passage through this gorgeous meadow. A bit smaller than its lower counterpart, Upper Gaylor Lake is backed by the striking form of Gaylor Peak, and it's every bit as photogenic as the middle lake. Stay with the pathway to the left along the shore, then follow it up the hillside, walking beside a tumbling waterway where bright yellow monkeyflowers cavort among the rounded stones.

Ascend steadily to reach the remnants of an old stone mining shack, evidence of the long-dead mining city of Dana. There are more shacks and mine shafts farther up the hill, but you may want to end your wandering here at the 2.0-mile point and linger to enjoy the matchless view.

You can simply return the way you came up, or, if you're good with a map and in the mood for a little variety, a bit of easy cross-country rambling will take you back via the oft-overlooked Granite Lakes, just to the west. These twin beauties offer scenic, if frigid, opportunities for some alpine swimming.

# CHAPTER FOUR

• • • • • • • •

# Yosemite East (Highway 395)

Highway 395 is California's north-south conduit along the eastern flank of the Sierra Nevada Mountains. This busy thoroughfare climbs from the desertlike expanses of the Owens River Valley to the lofty ski hills of Mammoth Lakes to the forested heights of the 7,519-foot Devils Gate Summit before continuing north into Nevada. And all along the way, it offers spectacular views of the rugged eastern face of the Sierra Nevada.

*A family explores the trail below Burro Pass.*

Since this book is the northern volume of a two-book series on the Sierra Nevada Mountains, we've chosen our hikes for this section working north of what seems to be the logical breaking point between north and south on Highway 395. Whereas the trailheads to the south of the junction of Highway 395 and Yosemite's Highway 120 are popular with hikers from Los Angeles and the southern portion of the state, trailheads to the north of the junction (and all the way to Lake Tahoe) are generally frequented by residents of the Bay area.

The trailheads to the north of Highway 120 provide access to two different wilderness areas—the Hoover Wilderness and the Carson–Iceberg Wilderness. (Refer to chapter 5 for background on the Carson–Iceberg Wilderness.) The Hoover Wilderness lies just to the north of Yosemite National Park, with the bulk of its acreage administered by the Toiyabe National Forest.

You won't need permits for day hiking in either the Hoover or Carson–Iceberg wildernesses. However, for overnight permits, campground information, maps, or other assistance, contact one of the following offices: Inyo National Forest, Mono Lake Ranger District, PO Box 10, Lee Vining, California 93541 or Toiyabe National Forest, Bridgeport Ranger District, PO Box 595, Bridgeport, California 93517.

## CAMPGROUNDS

**Lee Vining Creek Campground** *(Hike 19, Mine Creek and Bennettville Mine; Hike 20, Saddlebag Lake and Lake Helen)* This pleasant county-administered campground on the banks of Lee Vining Creek is extremely popular with fishermen, and it serves as a last-gasp option for would-be Yosemite campers who can't find an empty site. As such, it's usually full to overflowing on the weekends, so come early Friday if you're hoping to claim a spot.

To reach Lee Vining Creek Campground, drive Highway 120 3.5 miles west of its junction with Highway 395 and turn into the signed campground. More than 50 sites for tents and motorhomes are strung out along the creek, offering picnic tables, fireplaces, and plenty of quaking aspen shade.

There is no drinking water at the campground, but there are non-flush toilets. Open April to October. No reservations. Moderate fee.

**Junction Campground** *(Hike 19, Mine Creek and Bennettville Mine; Hike 20, Saddlebag Lake and Lake Helen)* Junction Campground is a primitive campground near Tioga and Ellery lakes with 10 sites for tents or motorhomes. Partly because of its proximity to the eastern edge of Yosemite National Park, this humble campground is fre-

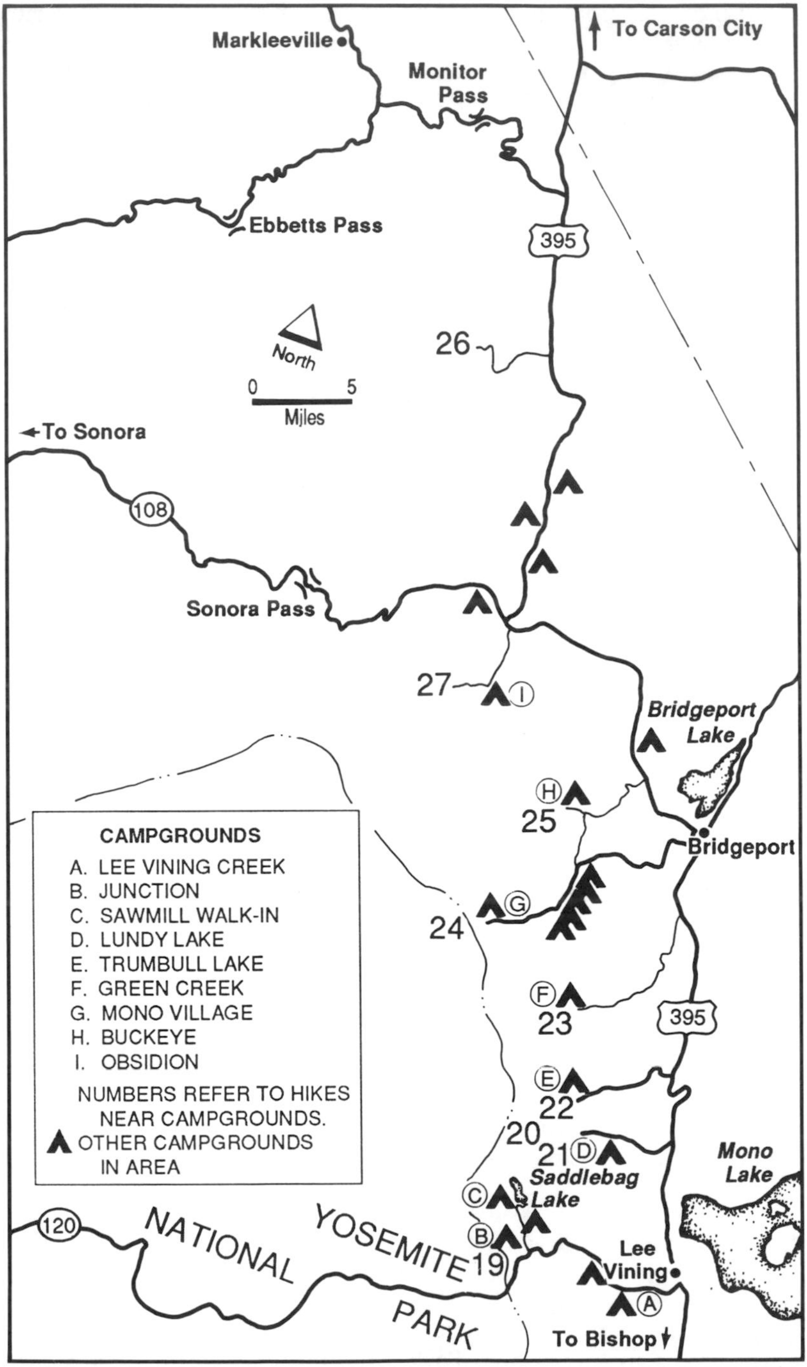

Markleeville •

Monitor
Pass

↑ To Carson City

Ebbetts Pass

395

26

North

0 _____ 5
Miles

← To Sonora

108

Sonora Pass

27

Ⓘ

Bridgeport
Lake

25

Ⓗ

Bridgeport

24

Ⓖ

**CAMPGROUNDS**

A. LEE VINING CREEK
B. JUNCTION
C. SAWMILL WALK-IN
D. LUNDY LAKE
E. TRUMBULL LAKE
F. GREEN CREEK
G. MONO VILLAGE
H. BUCKEYE
I. OBSIDION

NUMBERS REFER TO HIKES
NEAR CAMPGROUNDS.
▲ OTHER CAMPGROUNDS
IN AREA

Ⓕ
23

395

Ⓔ
22

20
21 Ⓓ

Mono
Lake

Ⓒ
Saddlebag
Lake

Ⓑ
19

Lee
Vining •

120

NATIONAL

YOSEMITE

PARK

Ⓐ

To Bishop ↓

quently full, so come early to claim your spot. This is a great place to stay if you're planning to check out Hike 19 as the trailhead is right in the camping area.

To reach Junction Campground, drive Highway 120 a short distance northeast of the Tioga Pass Summit and the Yosemite National Park entrance station, and watch for the signed Junction Campground on the north side of the road. There is no drinking water at Junction Campground, but there's a small cafe/store nearby.

Sites offer fireplaces and picnic tables, and non-flush toilets are available. Open June to October. No reservations. No fee.

**Sawmill Walk-in Campground** *(Hike 19, Mine Creek and Bennettville Mine; Hike 20, Saddlebag Lake and Lake Helen)* This is another surprisingly busy, primitive campground near the eastern entrance to Yosemite National Park. Sawmill Walk-in Campground's half dozen tent sites boast a spectacular setting with wonderful views of surrounding peaks.

To reach the campground, turn off Highway 120 northeast of the Yosemite National Park boundary at the sign for Saddlebag Lake. Drive 1.5 miles on an unpaved road to a sign for Sawmill Walk-in Campground. You'll have a 0.3- to 0.5-mile walk to your site from where you leave your car.

Non-flush toilets are available as well as picnic tables and fireplaces. There is no drinking water at Sawmill Walk-in Campground, however. Open June to October. No reservations. No fee.

**Lundy Lake Campground** *(Hike 21, Oneida Lake)*   This pleasant, shaded campground in Lundy Canyon offers 100 sites for tents and motorhomes. To find the county-run Lundy Lake Campground, turn off Highway 395 about 7.0 miles north of Lee Vining at the sign for Lundy Lake. Drive in 2.0 miles on a paved road to claim a site along Mill Creek.

There's no drinking water here, so you'll need to fill up before you come. Non-flush toilets, fireplaces, and picnic tables are provided for the roomy campspots. No reservations. Moderate fee.

**Trumbull Lake Campground** *(Hike 22, Burro Pass)* The midsized, often-crowded Trumbull Lake Campground is a great jumping-off point for the hike to Burro Pass. To reach the campground's 45 sites for tents and motorhomes, perched above popular Trumbull Lake, drive Highway 395 to Conway Summit (13.0 miles south of Bridgeport). Take the paved turnoff for Virginia Lakes. Drive in 5.7 miles and go right when the road branches to arrive at Trumbull Lake.

You'll want to have a good sleeping bag if you stay here, as the campground is set at a lofty 9,500 feet. The nights do get chilly.

Shaded sites offer drinking water, fireplaces, and picnic tables, and fishing options abound.

Trumbull Lake Campground is open June to October. Reservations available through (800) 280-CAMP. Moderate fee.

**Green Creek Campground** *(Hike 23, West Lake)*    This small, quiet campground boasts about a dozen campsites for tents or motorhomes. To reach Green Creek Campground and the start of the Green Creek Trail, turn west off Highway 395 about 4.5 miles south of Bridgeport. Drive on Green Creek Road (Road 142) for 9.0 miles to find your shaded site along Green Creek.

Drinking water is available, and campsites have picnic tables, fireplaces, and non-flush toilets. Green Creek Campground is open May to October. No reservations. Moderate fee.

**Mono Village Campground** *(Hike 24, Barney Lake)*    This huge camping "city" beside the upper of the two Twin Lakes not only contains the Barney Lake trailhead, but it also offers great access to the lake. Because of that, its more than 100 sites are crowded, noisy, and sadly overdeveloped. Recreational vehicles, boaters, and fishermen abound at the Mono Village Campground.

To reach the campground, turn off Highway 395 at Bridgeport for Twin Lakes. Drive in past the lower lake, then continue along the shoreline of the upper lake to arrive at Mono Village and the campground entrance.

Shaded spots here boast picnic tables, fireplaces, flush toilets, and drinking water. Trailer hookups are available, and there's a store and restaurant in Mono Village. Reservations are accepted for the privately operated campground, and you'll probably need one if you're arriving on a weekend. Moderate fee.

**Buckeye Campground** *(Hike 25, Big Meadow)*    It's an 11.3-mile drive to Buckeye Campground from Highway 395, but if you're walking to Big Meadow or planning to visit Buckeye Hot Springs, this is the spot to stay. To reach the campground, turn off Highway 395 at Bridgeport for Twin Lakes. Drive 7.7 miles to a junction signed for Buckeye Campground, and turn right onto unpaved Road 017. Drive to a second junction, and continue following signs for the campground.

The large and sprawling Buckeye Campground has 70 sites for tents and motorhomes. Drinking water and flush toilets are provided, and sites are equipped with picnic tables and fireplaces. Most of the sites aren't terribly attractive, however, so you'll want to pick and choose a bit.

One of the nicest things about Buckeye Campground is its proximity to Buckeye Hot Springs. These undeveloped hot springs provide a wonderful place to sit and soak hike-wearied muscles.

To find Buckeye Hot Springs, turn off Highway 395 at Bridgeport for Twin Lakes. Drive 7.7 miles to the junction signed for Buckeye Campground, and turn right onto unpaved Road 017. Drive to a second junction and go right again. Check your odometer here and continue 0.3 mile. Watch for an unsigned parking area beside the road, then descend on a very steep footpath to the banks of Buckeye Creek. Wonderful hot pools await.

The nearby Buckeye Campground is open May to October. No reservations. Moderate fee.

**Obsidian Campground** *(Hike 27, Emma Lake)*   This pleasant campground on Molybdenite Creek has 14 secluded campspots for tents or motorhomes. To find Obsidian Campground, leave Highway 395 0.7 mile south of the Sonora Junction, and drive south 3.5 miles on an unpaved road.

Quiet, shaded sites have picnic tables and fireplaces, but there is no drinking water. Non-flush toilets complete the rustic setting of Obsidian Campground. Open May to October. No reservations. Moderate fee.

## • • • • • • • • • • • •
# 19 MINE CREEK AND BENNETTVILLE MINE

Distance: 3.6 miles round trip
Difficulty: Easy
Starting point: 9,600 feet
High point: 9,900 feet
Map: USGS Tuolumne Meadows 15'

*Remnants of the Bennettville Mine operation*

This hike along flower-flanked Mine Creek to the site of the old Bennettville Mine is like taking a walk through a page of Sierra Nevada history. It is a relatively easy and a wonderful hike for children and wildflower lovers, and it offers fine views of Yosemite National Park's Mount Dana (Hike 13) along the way.

In 1882, some eager California businessmen transported 8 tons of mining equipment to the tiny settlement of Bennettville, hauling it in from the nearby town of Lundy via Saddlebag Lake (Hike 20). Thus began an ill-fated mining operation that was to end just 8 years later, without an ounce of silver ore ever being marketed. The Bennettville Mine did make a lasting mark on Sierra history,

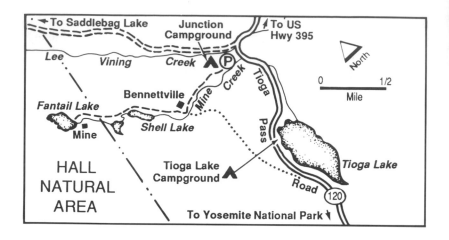

however, as the anticipated need for a better transportation route for supplies and ore contributed to construction of the old Tioga Road.

To reach the trailhead for Mine Creek, turn off Tioga Pass Road (Highway 120) northeast of the Yosemite National Park boundary at the sign for Junction Campground (near Tioga and Ellery lakes). Park near the entrance to Junction Campground. Be sure to pause at the historical plaque that tells the story of Bennettville and its mine.

Continue on foot into the campground. Just past Campsite No. 1, turn right to gain the signed Mine Creek Trail. Join the trail as it skirts up the hillside above the campground, and climb steadily along a rocky slope shaded by lodgepole and whitebark pines. The harsh terrain is host to many sturdy wildflowers—nude buckwheat, shieldleaf, and sulfur flower are just a few.

Cross a small stream, then hike above the rushing Mine Creek as you continue to ascend. You'll have fine views back toward Yosemite's Mount Dana whenever you pause to catch your breath. The incline mellows as the trail winds through a watery green meadow, then increases as it climbs beside the creek again.

Gain more level walking amid the wildflowers. Ranger buttons, cinquefoil, goldenrod, mariposa lily, and Indian paintbrush thrive in the moist conditions near the creek. You'll arrive at what's left of Bennettville at the 0.8-mile point. The "town" consists of two dilapidated wooden buildings and some warning signs aimed at would-be souvenir seekers.

To continue on to Shell Lake, regain the trail as it winds off to the left of a lightning-scarred lodgepole pine, and continue climbing with Mine Creek. Sniff the aroma of swamp onions and delight in the bright colors of Lemmon's paintbrush, hikers gentian, and cinquefoil.

Arrive at the shallow Shell Lake after 1.1 miles. You should be able to make out the traces of the old mine site on the hillside above (look for tailings on the slope). The detour to the mine is about a quarter of a mile. Otherwise, continue with the trail to the right along the shore of Shell Lake.

Reach a small pothole lake beyond Shell Lake, and look behind you for a wonderful view of Mount Dana. Pass an entry sign for the Hall Natural Area (no camping, no fires), and stay with the trail along the creek to arrive at Fantail Lake after 1.8 miles. Fantail Lake is a bit larger than Shell Lake, but its shallow center will disappoint would-be swimmers. Be content with some toe wiggling and wildflower watching if you're making this your stopping point. Mine Creek's course continues up a rapidly steepening canyon decorated with lovely wildflowers and waterfalls. It's definitely worth exploring if you have the time and energy.

# 20 SADDLEBAG LAKE AND LAKE HELEN

Distance: 8.4 miles (loop)
Difficulty: Moderate
Starting point: 10,080 feet
High point: 10,400 feet
Maps: USGS Tuolumne Meadows 15'
and USGS Matterhorn Peak 15'

*Delicate Coville's columbine*

This hike from Saddlebag Lake will take you through an alpine wonderland of heavenly scenery, crystal-clear lakes, and scores of wildflowers. This is a must-do hike for those exploring the Sierra landscape east of Yosemite. If you're strapped for time, however, you can cut 3.0 miles off this 8.4-mile loop by taking the shuttle boat to the far end of Saddlebag Lake and catching it again on your return (cost is about $5 per person).

To reach the trailhead for Lake Helen, turn off Tioga Pass Road (Highway 120) northeast of the Yosemite National Park boundary at the sign for Saddlebag Lake. Drive 2.5 miles on unpaved road and watch for the "trailhead parking" sign that designates the hikers' parking lot.

If you're opting for the shuttle boat, continue on foot to the

*An old mining road traces a portion of the route to Lake Helen.*

small cafe/store on the lakefront. There's a campground here as well as drinking water and toilets.

Otherwise, walk downhill toward the dam as you leave the parking lot. If the spillway is empty, you can cross on top. Otherwise, take the roadway crossing just below the dam and set out on the trail along the shore of sprawling Saddlebag Lake. The lower path is a use trail for fishermen, so stick with the upper route.

The trail is quite rocky, yet an amazing variety of wildflowers manages to thrive beside the lake. Watch for ranger buttons, alpine goldenrod, and Coville's columbine. Continue on the level path, and gain a view of Shepherd Crest as you round the bend.

The ground is colorful with Lemmon's paintbrush, Indian paintbrush, and little elephant heads near the far end of the lake. Stay with the trail as you climb away from the water and take in a view of pretty Greenstone Lake ahead (1.5-mile point).

The trail peters out a bit in this section. Angle right about 100 yards short of Greenstone Lake to find a rock crossing of the outlet creek (you may have to wade in early season). Then continue beside the creek to reach the shore of Greenstone Lake.

Follow the shoreline to the right and merge with the trail coming up from the Saddlebag Lake boat landing. You'll have fine views of Mount Conness and the Conness Glacier to the left of North Peak as you begin climbing away from Greenstone Lake, then gain an old mining road to continue your ascent.

The steady uphill route is lined with whitebark and lodgepole pines. Pass an entry sign for the Hall Natural Area (no camping, no fires), and enjoy a letup in the incline for a while. Descend to the edge of Wasco Lake, angling right with the old mining road. A view of deep Steelhead Lake appears as you continue.

If you're looking for an early stopping point, you can take the trail to the left to reach a small waterfall and a swimming area on the lovely, 10,300-foot Steelhead Lake (the 2.9-mile point). Otherwise, take the trail to the right along the shore and enjoy fine views of Mount Conness and North Peak above the lake.

Curve right with the road at the far end of the lake, and wind through rocky terrain to reach a smaller lake (on the right) at the 3.3-mile point. Abandon the old mining road to cross a creek and gain a footpath along the far side of the lake. Then stay with the trail as you press on toward enchanting Shamrock Lake, a deep jewel highlighted with a handful of small rock islands.

Cross a stream lined with monkeyflowers and California corn lily, then skirt along a rocky slope. Continue on past scattered whitebark pines. The trail is difficult to follow here, so keep to the right and watch for ducks as you hike above Lake Helen.

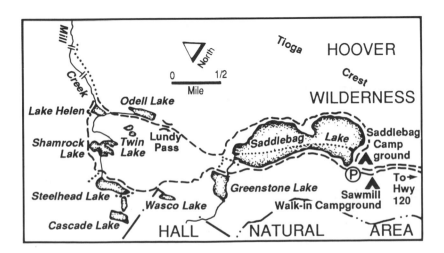

Descend a steep slope and scramble across a hillside aflame with fireweed. At 4.4 miles you gain the far end of Lake Helen. Cross the small outlet stream on a stone causeway, then go right on a rocky trail overhung with an abundance of delicate Coville's columbine.

Follow the lakeshore to a narrow canyon, awash in yellow monkeyflower, and ascend the canyon beside a tumbling creek. This section of the trail can retain its snow quite late into the season, so be very careful with your footing here. If you're hiking after the snows have slipped down into Lake Helen, you'll be enthralled by alpine shooting star, alpine goldenrod, Lemmon's paintbrush, and a lot of monkeyflowers as you climb.

When the canyon begins to level out, abandon the creek and gain a trail along the slope to the right. Arrive at Odell Lake not long afterward. Follow the trail along the lakeshore, then climb to Lundy Pass. Look for the handsome form of Mount Dana straight ahead, and begin descending through a green valley, passing tiny Hummingbird Lake along the way.

Reach a sign for the Hoover Wilderness and regain sight of Saddlebag Lake. Descend gently toward the distant shoreline and angle left when you reach an old roadway paralleling the lakeshore the 6.0-mile point). If you'd like a quicker return route, the trail to the right, which you began on, is about 0.5 mile shorter. Otherwise, continue to the left around the lake, enjoying an easy walk on the mostly level roadway.

• • • • • • • • • • • • • • • • • • • • • • • •

# 21   ONEIDA LAKE

Distance: 7.0 miles round trip
Difficulty: Strenuous
Starting point: 7,810 feet
High point: 9,650 feet
Maps: USGS Lundy 7.5' and USGS Mount Dana 7.5'

This pleasant but challenging hike to Oneida Lake offers a glimpse into the mining history of the Sierra Nevada. Sections of the trail follow the old mining road that led to the May Lundy Mine. Watch for the skeletons of discarded mining equipment on the way to Oneida Lake, now a popular destination for backpackers.

To find the trailhead for Oneida Lake, turn off Highway 395 about 7.0 miles north of Lee Vining at the sign for Lundy Lake. Drive in 3.5 miles and take the turnoff for the Lundy Hydroelectric

*Abandoned tram tracks of an old mining operation, Oneida Lake*

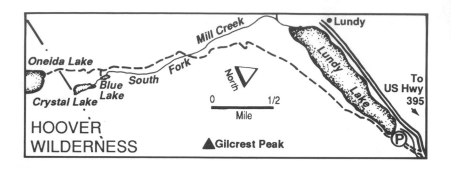

Project. Follow the gravel road to its end at a small parking area and trailhead sign.

Begin on a trail signed for Crystal, Oneida, and Ada lakes, following the aspen-lined shore of Lundy Lake. With a resort at one end and deep water for fishermen, Lundy Lake draws its share of visitors on a weekend day. You'll have mule ears and woolly mullein for company as you tread the old mining road along the shore.

The way is level at first, then the road climbs along the hillside at a steady incline. Watch for deer tracks in the dirt, and savor the widening panorama as you gain elevation. Mountain pennyroyal, Indian paintbrush, sulfur flower, nude buckwheat, and tower larkspur line the way.

Pass the end of Lundy Lake and continue climbing, crossing a small stream where ranger buttons, alpine monkeyflower, and monkshood thrive on a thin trickle of water. Turn uphill with the road as it curves to ascend a rocky canyon trimmed with the white ribbon of an alpine waterfall.

The climb mellows at the 2-mile point. Find the chortling South Fork of Mill Creek 0.2 mile farther. The banks are crowded with tower larkspur, fireweed, broadleaf lupine, and alpine goldenrod, but the cool air above the water is an even better reason to linger.

Continue climbing gently, then ascend more steeply for 0.5 mile. The incline eases as the trail traverses a green alpine meadow where a host of wild irises turn their faces toward the sun. Watch for petite Blue Lake on the left at 2.9 miles. The way branches soon after, with the trail to the left leading to Crystal Lake (0.3 mile farther). Remnants of the defunct mining settlement huddle along its shore.

Stay with the main branch straight ahead and climb steadily to look down onto Crystal Lake. Mine tailings are evident on the hillside to the right, where the spine of Tioga Ridge traces the old route to the mining town of Bennettville (Hike 19).

Reach a set of derelict tram tracks at 3.3 miles. You'll spot a lot of rusted mining equipment in the valley down below, and there's a closed off mine shaft to the right. The old mining road is replaced by a footpath that leads on to the shore of Oneida Lake. Pass an entry sign for the Hoover Wilderness along the way.

Reach Oneida Lake at 3.5 miles. With shallow edges and a deep center, the lake is cold yet tantalizing, rimmed by harsh red-rocked slopes. Lunch with the ghosts of long-dead miners, then turn back toward civilization.

• • • • • • • • • • • • • • • • • • • • • • • • • • •

# 22 BURRO PASS

Distance: 5.8 miles round trip
Difficulty: Strenuous
Starting point: 9,760 feet
High point: 11,150 feet
Map: USGS Matterhorn Peak 15'

Of all the hikes accessible from Highway 395, this climb to the crest of Burro Pass ranks as one of the most impressive. The views from the summit are nothing short of spectacular, and the scenery along the way will take the edge off the effort of the long ascent.

To reach the trailhead for Burro Pass, drive Highway 395 to Conway Summit (13.0 miles south of Bridgeport), then take the paved turnoff for Virginia Lakes. Drive in 5.7 miles and follow signs for the trailhead, angling left and then right. (It's also possible to take a trail that leaves from Trumbull Lake Campground.)

Start out from the parking area, following an old roadbed along the ridge. To the left is a view of the large Virginia Lake. Dive off the ridge to gain the forested ravine on the right. The trail through the ravine is shaded by lodgepole pines.

Reach an entry sign for the Hoover Wilderness. The trail branches soon after, but both branches merge again. Pass deep Blue Lake on the left, and tread a trail lined with mountain penny-royal, fireweed, and scarlet gilia.

Climb away from Blue Lake on a rocky trail, ascending steadily as you pass the 0.5-mile point. You'll wind through an alpine meadow knee-deep in California corn lily and colorful leopard lily, and come to an old log cabin at 1.0 mile.

Ascend another rocky slope to arrive at Cooney Lake after 1.2 miles. From here, you'll have a view of Burro Pass ahead. Wind along the shore of Cooney Lake, watching for the blossoms of Sierra arnica, spirea, and fragrant mountain pennyroyal. The lake has a pretty shoreline with steep dropoffs that make tempting diversions for swimmers.

Leave Cooney Lake and climb beside a shallow stream, keeping an eye out for a trail angling left across the water. The trail continuing straight ahead appears to be the main branch, but it's not. Cross the stream and arrive at the first petite member of the Frog Lakes family after 0.1 mile (the lake will be on your right).

The shoreline is decorated with an enchanting blend of Lemmon's paintbrush, hikers gentian, little elephant heads, and meadow penstemon. Hike onward through a chain of tiny lakes, enjoying level going and a plethora of wildflowers.

The ascent is steady and somewhat steep as you resume climbing past stunted whitebark pines. As you gain elevation there is a nice view down onto Frog Lakes. The grade increases with a set

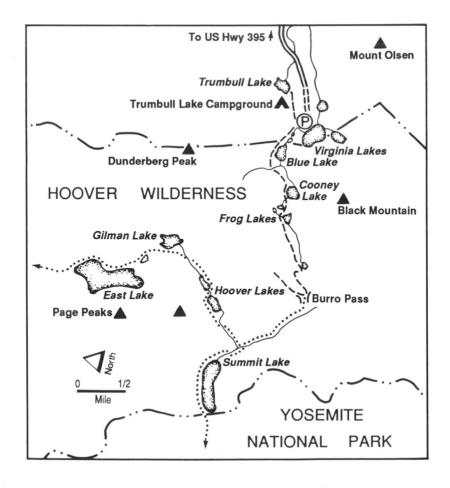

*The view from Burro Pass is nothing short of spectacular.*

of switchbacks, and the handsome form of Black Mountain rules a jagged ridge of cliffs reminiscent of cathedral spires.

Reach the windswept summit of 11,110-foot Burro Pass at 2.9 miles. The view from here is striking. To the east, you'll see the Mono Valley and a distant line of mountains. As you continue up and over the Burro Pass ridgeline, leave the trail to scramble up the rocky slope to the right, where there is a fantastic view in all directions.

To the west, look for Summit Lake, backed by 12,000-foot Virginia Peak. To the right of Summit Lake, Hoover Lake and East Lake nestle in the valley floor. A wall of mountains rears beyond the lakes, and the sight of their rugged shapes against a blue Sierra sky is a picture that will make the challenging climb to Burro Pass seem like one of the best energy investments you've ever made.

• • • • • • • • • • • • • • • • • • • • • • • • •

# 23 WEST LAKE

Distance: 7.4 miles round trip
Difficulty: Strenuous
Starting point: 8,000 feet
High point: 9,900 feet
Map: USGS Matterhorn Peak 15'

This popular route along the Green Creek Trail offers a wealth of hiking options and a fistful of alluring alpine lakes. You'll share the way with scores of backpackers if you're hiking on a weekend day, but the many trail options scatter the crowds quite effectively.

To reach the start of the Green Creek Trail, turn west off Highway 395 about 4.5 miles south of Bridgeport. Drive on Green Creek Road (Road 142) for 9.4 miles, following signs for the trail 0.4 mile beyond Green Creek Campground. (In 1988, hikers were rerouted to begin from a temporary trailhead, 0.9 mile short of the original trailhead. The round-trip mileage noted above is based on the original trailhead.)

Begin walking beneath lodgepole and Jeffrey pines, Sierra junipers, and quaking aspens, following the course of Green Creek as you go. Climb steadily for 0.2 mile, then descend briefly to a more level walk going past broadleaf lupine, sage, Indian paintbrush, and mountain mahogany.

Resume climbing beside the water, frothy white in its tumbling descent, and work your way through a series of tough switchbacks before the grade mellows a little bit. Reach an entry sign for the Hoover Wilderness at the 1.0-mile point. Continue beside the creek, watching for beaver dams and ponds through the white trunks of the quaking aspens.

Enter a more open area where fireweed, tower larkspur, common monkeyflower, yarrow, and ranger buttons clamor for the sun. Look for Gabbro Peak ahead (slightly to the left), and climb gently as you continue on. Cross a vast slide area after 2.0 miles. The larger trees have been swept away, to be replaced by quaking aspens, sage, and a tangle of underbrush.

Arrive at a junction at 2.1 miles. You can go left for Green Lake (if you'd like to make a shorter day of it—0.3 mile from the junction). Otherwise, go right for West Lake, climbing steadily up the hillside to gain a view of Green Lake from above.

The grade increases as the trail traces switchbacks up the hill. Cross a creek overwhelmed with cinquefoil, tower larkspur, broadleaf lupine, and ranger buttons, then continue climbing in switch-

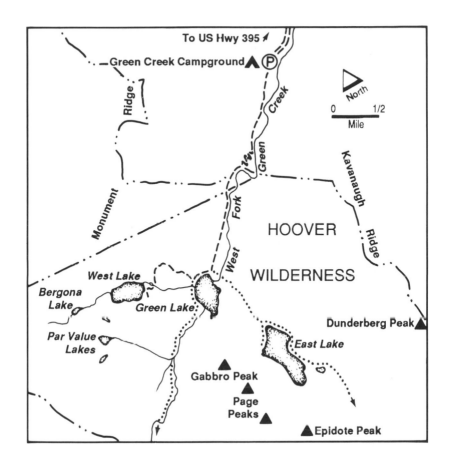

backs with patches of bright yellow Sierra arnica to cheer you on the way.

You'll reach an overlook spot on the ridge just before the summit of the climb (3.4-mile point). Pause for a fine view down onto Green Lake, and gain a peek at the corner of East Lake just over the ridge beyond. Enjoy a vista to the east of the Green Creek Canyon as well.

Continue to the crest of the ridge, descend to cross a creek, then angle right along the shore of a small pond to reach the edge of West Lake after 3.7 miles. Ringed by rocky cliffs that seem to tumble right into the water, West Lake is deep and cold and lovely, a popular destination spot for backpackers and day hikers.

Spread your picnic in the shade of one of the stunted pines that huddle on the shore and soak in the scenery of this alpine gem until your eyes are satiated and your legs are rested.

● ● ● ● ● ● ● ● ● ● ● ● ● ● ● ● ● ● ● ● ● ● ● ● ● ●

# 24   BARNEY LAKE

Distance: 8.4 miles round trip
Difficulty: Moderate
Starting point: 7,120 feet
High point: 8,300 feet
Map: USGS Matterhorn Peak 15'

The Mono Village Campground provides excellent access to this pleasant hike to Barney Lake, but even if you're staying somewhere else, this trail is worth exploring. To reach the trailhead, turn off Highway 395 at Bridgeport for Twin Lakes. Drive in past the lower lake, then continue along the shoreline of the upper lake, feasting your eyes on one of the finest roadside views you'll find in the Sierra Nevada—the Sawtooth Ridge above Twin Lakes.

Enter Mono Village and park at the boat launch area. Daytime parking in Mono Village is free, but overnighters must pay $5. There's a store and cafe here as well as hordes of fishermen, boaters, and campers.

Begin walking with a 0.3-mile stroll through the camping area, following signs for Barney Lake Trail. Reach an old fire road and continue walking, watching for a trail veering off to the right soon after (it's signed). Angle right on the Barney Lake Trail, and walk through a shady forest of Jeffrey pines, white firs, and Fremont cottonwoods.

Trade your level walking for gentle climbing after 0.8 mile. The voice of Robinson Creek will keep you company. Angle left to cross a small stream, and continue climbing through more open ground, sprinkled with mule ears and sage.

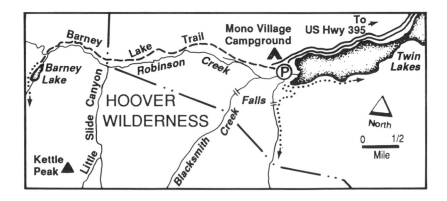

You'll enter a large, sun-drenched valley sprinkled with Sierra junipers as you continue a gentle ascent beside the water. Watch for beaver ponds glistening between the trunks of quaking aspens. Just before the entry sign for the Hoover Wilderness (2.7 miles) there is a fine view to the left of the rugged Little Slide Canyon.

Walk beside the creek awhile longer, then turn uphill and climb more steeply. The sweet aroma of wild roses mingles with the pungent smell of mountain pennyroyal. Gain a view back toward Twin Lakes as the altitude increases, then cross a creek knee-deep in monkshood, ranger buttons, and alpine goldenrod.

The incline mellows at 3.6 miles. There is a final, short, rocky slope to negotiate in several switchbacks, then the trail winds on through a shaded forest to reach the shore of Barney Lake at 4.2 miles. As you gaze southwest across the water, spot the 11,346-foot Crown Point in the center of your panorama.

With a sandy beach that's wonderful for wading and a ring of steep granite slopes to make it scenic, Barney Lake is a great place to laze away a sunny summer afternoon. Pull off your shoes and wiggle your toes awhile.

## 25 BIG MEADOW

Distance: 8 miles round trip
Difficulty: Easy
Starting point: 7,200 feet
High point: 7,600 feet
Map: USGS Matterhorn Peak 15'

*A toppled quaking aspen is a beaver's calling card.*

If you're visiting the Sierra early in the hiking season and searching for a hike that will be clear of the retreating snows, this relatively easy walk to Big Meadow is worth checking out. One advantage of doing this hike early in the summer is that you'll be sure to catch its crop of meadow wildflowers before late-summer hordes of grazing cattle move in to mow them down.

Sections of this hike traverse private land and cross several fencelines. Please be sure to latch all gates behind you. This will ensure continuing good relations with the landowners and, therefore, continuing opportunities to take this walk.

To reach the trailhead for Big Meadow, turn off Highway 395

at Bridgeport for Twin Lakes. Drive 7.7 miles to a junction signed for Buckeye Campground, and turn right onto unpaved Road 017. Drive to a second junction and continue following signs for Buckeye Campground for a total of 3.6 miles on unpaved roads.

Once at the campground, continue an additional 0.6 mile to reach a sign for the Buckeye Trail and the start of your hike to Big Meadow. Enter through a gate on the left side of the fence and begin walking on a sandy road beneath Jeffrey pines.

The ground beneath the trees is dry and open in late summer, but the way is colorful with broadleaf lupine early in the year. You'll begin to hear the whisper of Buckeye Creek after about 0.5 mile, and quaking aspens move in to join the pines.

Wind on through thicker stands of Jeffrey pines, and sniff the

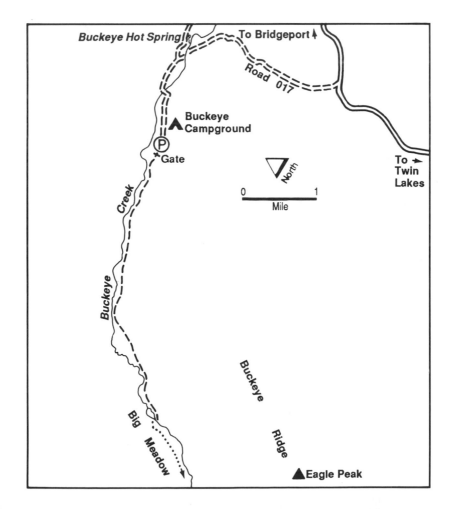

*The Big Meadow hike boasts sweeping views and mellow walking.*

telltale scent of sage as you continue. Large cones and deep piles of pine needles are scattered on the ground beneath the trees. Reach a barbed-wire fence at 1.2 miles. There's a gate on the left side.

This fence marks the border of the first small meadow, edged with quaking aspens and Sierra junipers. In the center, countless wild iris blossoms turn their faces toward the sun. Look for a host of other meadow wildflowers—yarrow, yampah, cinquefoil, and Sierra arnica.

Walk on through sage and mule ears, and watch for the delicate blossoms of scarlet gilia. The road narrows to a footpath as you reenter trees, then the terrain is transformed into meadowland again. Arrive at the largest meadow yet at the 2.2-mile point.

You'll begin to pick up views of the mountains a short distance later. To the left, Buckeye Ridge is ruled by Eagle Peak and Victoria Peak. Look for a sign for the Buckeye Trail at the edge of another broad meadow at 2.8 miles. From here, you'll have the finest view of the mountains this hike has to offer. If you're looking for an early stopping point, this is it.

Angle left into the shelter of the trees as you skirt along the edge of the meadow. If you have children along, be sure to point out the evidence of resident beavers—toppled aspen trees with their trunks whittled into pencil points.

Rejoin Buckeye Creek briefly, then climb to cross a low forested ridge ruled by Sierra junipers and Jeffrey pines. Big Meadow appears as you descend. The meadow stretches, green and open, for more than a mile, with the distant mountains acting as an impressive backdrop.

Reach Buckeye Creek at the 4.0-mile point in your walk. The edge of the meadow is fenced, but there's a trail sign and a gate to the right (across the creek). Wade the little waterway if you want to explore the wide open spaces beyond. Otherwise, savor the scenery and the flowers before you turn for home.

● ● ● ● ● ● ● ● ● ● ● ● ● ● ● ● ● ● ● ● ● ● ● ● ●

# 26 RODRIGUEZ FLAT

Distance: 2.6 miles round trip
Difficulty: Easy
Starting point: 8,200 feet
High point: 8,800 feet
Map: USGS Coleville 7.5′

This short hike is noteworthy for its views of the rugged peaks of the Carson–Iceberg Wilderness, and it's a nice excursion when you're looking for an easy jaunt to stretch your legs. The drive in to the trailhead is less than inviting, however, so if you're uncom-

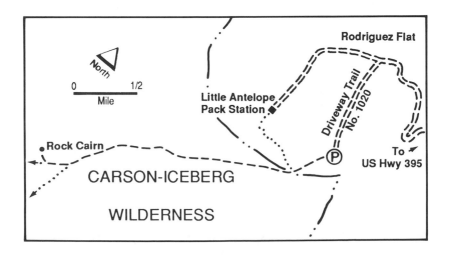

*Vistas of the Carson–Iceberg Wilderness enhance the hike to Rodriguez Flat.*

fortable with steep hills and rough, unpaved roads, try another hike.

To reach the trailhead for Rodriguez Flat, drive 2.0 miles north of Walker on Highway 395. Turn west onto Mill Canyon Road, and follow signs for Little Antelope Pack Station/Rodriguez Flats. The unpaved road is extremely steep, and it's definitely not a thoroughfare for cars with a tendency to overheat.

Drive in 6.4 miles, then turn left at a sign for "Driveway Trail No. 1020." The final 0.5 mile of road is studded with rocks and holes, so you may want to park a little early and walk to the trailhead. If you're hiking on a weekend, you'll probably share your way with a lot of horses, as this is a popular packers' route into the Carson–Iceberg Wilderness.

Leave the small parking area and begin walking gently uphill in the shade of quaking aspens and white firs. Broadleaf lupine, mule ears, and sage scramble for moisture in the parched Sierra soil. Arrive at a junction with the trail from the Little Antelope Pack Station after 0.3 mile.

Continue on past an entry sign for the Carson–Iceberg Wilderness, and begin climbing in earnest. Lodgepole pines, western white pines, and white firs give way to more open terrain as you ascend. But scarlet gilia, mountain pennyroyal, sulfur flower, and Indian paintbrush take over where the trees leave off.

Enjoy expanding views as you continue climbing. The grade mellows at 0.8 mile, and you'll have a vista to the west of several peaks in the Carson–Iceberg Wilderness. Reach the crest of the hill and begin a gentle descent. Straight ahead (to the southwest), you'll see a row of mountains ruled by Whitecliff Peak.

Reach a trail sign and a junction at 1.2 miles, and pause to read the explanatory sign about this region's famous Piute trout. Take the pathway on the right to make your way toward a large rock cairn visible 0.1 mile farther on. The ridgetop is ruled by sage and mule ears, with the bright colors of Indian paintbrush and sulfur flower mixed in.

Abandon the trail to cut through sageland toward the cairn, and reach your goal at 1.3 miles. This structure built of piled rocks offers a great picnic spot and a fine vista. Pull up a patch of open ground and feast your eyes while you munch.

● ● ● ● ● ● ● ● ● ● ● ● ● ● ● ● ● ● ● ● ● ● ● ● ● ● ● ●

# 27 EMMA LAKE

Distance: 2.2 miles round trip
Difficulty: Easy
Starting point: 8,560 feet
High point: 9,300 feet
Map: USGS Fales Hot Springs 7.5'

This short jaunt to Emma Lake makes a wonderful family excursion for a noontime picnic and/or an afternoon dip. The trail has some steep sections, but they're mercifully short, and Emma Lake is a worthy goal.

To reach the trailhead for Emma Lake, leave Highway 395 0.7 mile south of the Sonora junction. Drive 3.5 miles on an unpaved road to Obsidian Campground, then continue another 3.5 miles to

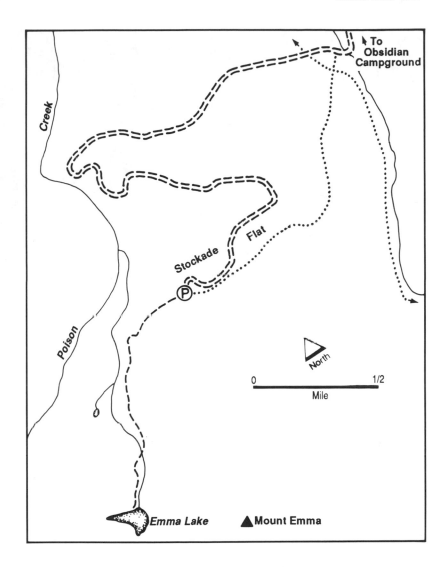

the road's end and a sign proclaiming the trail closed to all motor vehicles.

Start out from the small parking area and begin climbing immediately. The forest is studded with massive red fir stumps, and living red firs and lodgepole pines cast their shadows on the trail. Mule ears, sage, and mountain pennyroyal give witness to the dryness of the soil.

Climb steeply to the 0.5-mile point, then enjoy easier going as you wind across an open flat with wild iris, cinquefoil, and yarrow

*Pretty Emma Lake plays host to grazing sheep in August.*

for your wildflower companions. Begin climbing once again, ascending beside a tumbling stream.

Cross the little waterway and scramble up an open, rock-strewn hillside to arrive at Emma Lake at 1.1 miles. Steep, rocky slopes form a lovely semicircle around this deep blue lake. It's popular with fishermen and has good depth for swimming. Choose a spot along the shore and spread your picnic or your towel.

# CHAPTER FIVE

• • • • • • • • •

# Sonora Pass (Highway 108)

Sonora Pass is the first road crossing the Sierra Nevada north of Yosemite's Tioga Pass. A pack animal route was established across this rugged section of the Sierra in 1862, negotiating the present-day Saint Marys Pass (Hike No. 36). But this route proved to be too difficult, and the Sonora-Mono Toll Road was built later in the decade as a supply route for the eastern mining towns of Aurora and Bodie. That road followed much of the course of today's Highway 108.

The treacherous, curving route known as Sonora Pass was no favorite of nineteenth-century pioneers, and it remains a challenge to twentieth-century travelers today. Gruesomely steep grades, hairpin turns, and narrow passageways between rock cliffs make this an exceedingly difficult pass to negotiate. Don't plan on setting any land speed records for your Sierra passage, if you choose to use Sonora Pass. But do plan on numerous far-ranging vistas, filled with exquisite mountain scenery.

The Sonora Pass Road slices between two California wilderness areas. The Emigrant Wilderness lies to the south of Highway 108, offering more than 100,000 acres of forestland, granite slopes, lovely lakes, and flower-bedecked meadows. The Emigrant Wilderness is named for the thousands of hearty travelers who braved the Sierra Nevada on their journey to the promised land of California. The Clark-Skidmore party was the first emigrant group to use the West Walker route over Emigrant Pass, making the difficult passage in 1852. They were followed by several other emigrant groups, and anyone interested in pioneer history will surely find the Emigrant Wilderness a fascinating place to explore.

To the north of Highway 108, the Carson–Iceberg Wilderness is composed of 160,000 acres of pristine Sierra high country. Roughly 78,000 acres of this wilderness are within the Stanislaus National Forest (along with all of the Emigrant Wilderness), whereas the remaining acres are part of the Toiyabe National Forest. What the Carson–Iceberg Wilderness lacks in accessible alpine lakes, it makes up for in wilderness solitude, and it's definitely the

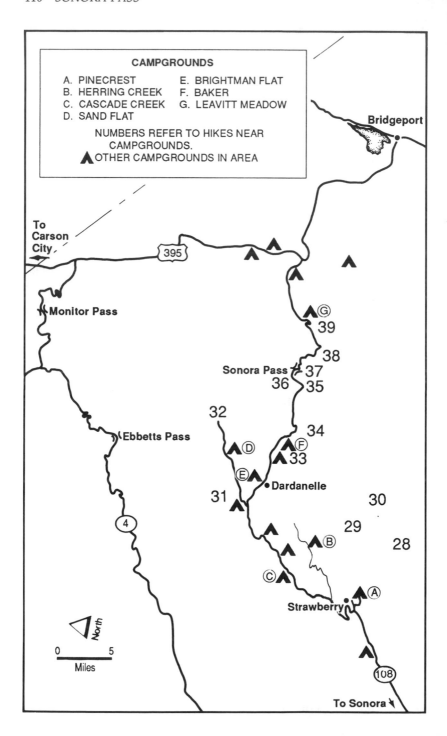

CAMPGROUNDS

A. PINECREST        E. BRIGHTMAN FLAT
B. HERRING CREEK    F. BAKER
C. CASCADE CREEK    G. LEAVITT MEADOW
D. SAND FLAT

NUMBERS REFER TO HIKES NEAR
CAMPGROUNDS.
▲OTHER CAMPGROUNDS IN AREA

Bridgeport

To Carson City

395

Monitor Pass

39

38

Sonora Pass   37
36           35

32

Ebbetts Pass

34

33

31

Dardanelle

30

29

28

4

B

C

Strawberry

A

North

0        5
Miles

108

To Sonora

place to go if you're seeking refuge from the crowds at Yosemite or Tahoe.

If you intend to use the hikes in this section as day hikes, you won't need a wilderness permit for either the Emigrant or Carson–Iceberg Wilderness. For overnight hikes, you must obtain a permit. West of Sonora Pass Summit, permits can be requested at the Summit Ranger District office, located just beyond the Pinecrest Lake turnoff, about 30 miles from Sonora. Mail permit requests to Summit Ranger District, Star Route 1295, Sonora, California 95370.

East of Sonora Pass Summit, contact the Carson Ranger District, 1536 S Carson Street, Carson City, Nevada 89701.

## CAMPGROUNDS

**Pinecrest Campground** (*Hike 28, Burst Rock and Powell Lake*)  A scenic setting on Pinecrest Lake makes the sprawling Pinecrest Campground an exceedingly busy place. Make reservations if you want a weekend site, despite the 200 spots for tents and motorhomes.

To reach the campground, turn off Highway 108 for Pinecrest, and drive 0.6 mile to the campground entrance. Drinking water, flush toilets, picnic tables, and fireplaces are available, and there's an easy trail around Pinecrest Lake that's accessible from here as well. Open May to October. Reservations available through (800) 280-CAMP. Moderate fee.

**Herring Creek Campground** (*Hike 29, Waterhouse Lake; Hike 30, Horse and Cow Meadow*)  To reach this quiet, primitive campground, turn off Highway 108, 2.3 miles east of Strawberry, and follow Herring Creek Road toward Herring Creek Reservoir. Drive 4.5 miles on paved road, then another 2.5 miles to a junction for the reservoir. The campground is on the left, near the small Herring Creek Reservoir.

If you camp here on a weekday, you may be all alone, as the campground's location and limited facilities discourage crowds. The setting is pleasant, and the 20-plus sites are well shaded, with picnic tables and fireplaces. The road in is rough, so the campground is best suited for tents or small camper units.

If you do make the trip off Highway 108 to Herring Creek Campground, be sure to visit the Trail of the Gargoyles. This fascinating walk is a bit too short to be listed as a full-scale hike in this book, but you can cover almost 2.0 miles if you make the entire tour of the delightful geologic formations called the Gargoyles.

You'll spot a sign for the Trail of the Gargoyles on your way to Herring Creek Campground, 6.8 miles from Highway 108. Drive in 0.2 mile on the rough entry road. Be sure to pick up a printed pamphlet from the metal box beside the trailhead before you begin.

*A father and son share a snack near the shore of Powell Lake.*

The trail is easy to follow, but it does run along exposed slopes, so be very careful with children.

Herring Creek Campground offers non-flush toilets, but there is no drinking water. Open June to October. No reservations. No fee.

**Cascade Creek Campground** (*Hike 29, Waterhouse Lake; Hike 30, Horse and Cow Meadow*)   Although it's right on Highway 108, Cascade Creek Campground is an often lonely spot. As such, it's a delightful place to camp. Tall trees tower above the handful of undeveloped tentsites near little Cascade Creek. Some sites are large enough for motorhomes. There are fireplaces and non-flush toilets here, but there's no drinking water. Picnic tables are conspicuously absent.

To find the campground, drive 9.0 miles east of Strawberry on Highway 108, and watch for the sign for Cascade Creek Campground. Not far beyond Cascade Creek Campground (6.0 miles farther east on Highway 108) is the well-signed Donnell Vista, where an easy 10-minute walk on an asphalt path leads to an impressive overlook of the Donnell Reservoir. Interesting historical plaques line the way, and the vista of the reservoir and the distant Dardanelles is more than worth the walk.

Cascade Creek Campground is a great option if you're searching for a campspot on a busy weekend. Open June to October. No reservations. No fee.

**Sand Flat Campground** *(Hike 31, Sword Lake; Hike 32, Boulder Creek)* Turn off Highway 108 at the sign for Clark Fork (about 19.0 miles east of the Summit Ranger Station), and drive 6.3 miles on the paved Clark Fork Road to reach the sprawling Sand Flat Campground. Shaded by tall Jeffrey pines, this is a roomy spot for family camping.

Its 50 campsites offer picnic tables, fireplaces, and non-flush toilets. Drinking water is available at the campground, and there is a resident campground host. Sand Flat Campground is open May to October. No reservations. Moderate fee.

**Brightman Flat Campground** *(Hike 33, Giant Jeffrey Walk)* This un-assuming campground is 1.0 mile west of Dardanelle on Highway 108. With 30 sites for tents or motorhomes, Brightman Flat Campground overlooks the lovely Stanislaus River. This scenic spot is extremely popular with fishermen. Arrive early Friday afternoon to claim a weekend site.

Be sure to make the short excursion to view the Columns of the Giants if you're staying at Brightman Flat. This 0.5-mile round-trip walk is accessible from the picnic area beside the Pidgeon Flat Campground on Highway 108, 4.4 miles east of the Clark Fork Road junction or 3.4 miles west of the Kennedy Meadow turnoff. The easy, level walk yields a view of a group of 40-foot-high basalt columns, formed 150,000 years ago by volcanic eruptions.

There is no drinking water at Brightman Flat Campground, so fill containers at Dardanelle or the nearby ranger station. Picnic tables and fireplaces are provided, and there are non-flush toilets available. With its riverbank setting, this free campground is a treat. It's open May to October. No reservations. Moderate fee.

**Baker Campground** *(Hike 34, Relief Reservoir Viewpoint; Hike 35, Blue Canyon; Hike 36, Saint Marys Pass and Sonora Peak; Hike 37, Sonora Pass Trailhead)* This sprawling campground has more than 40 sites for tents or motorhomes. Reach Baker Campground from Highway 108 at the Kennedy Meadow turnoff, 5.5 miles southeast of Dardanelle. Located on the Stanislaus River, the shaded campground is often crowded and less than idyllic, especially on weekends.

Sites have picnic tables and fireplaces, and the campground offers drinking water and non-flush toilets. Baker Campground is open May to October. No reservations. Moderate fee.

**Leavitt Meadow Campground** *(Hike 38, Sardine Falls; Hike 39, Secret Lake)* With a pleasant situation on the West Walker River, the midsized Leavitt Meadow Campground offers 16 shaded sites for tents or motorhomes, complete with picnic tables, fireplaces, drinking water, and non-flush toilets. Reach Leavitt Meadow Campground from Highway 108, 8.0 miles east of Sonora Pass Summit and 7.0 miles west of Highway 395.

Not only is the trailhead for Secret Lake (Hike 39) only 0.2 mile from the campground, this is also a good base for making the drive to the Leavitt Falls overlook, just 1.7 miles west on Highway 108. Watch carefully for the unsigned turnoff for the falls. Pull off onto the unpaved spur road on the south side of the highway. Then walk west down the rough roadway, gain a footpath, and continue a short distance to a viewpoint of Leavitt Falls.

The slope here is steep and dangerous, so keep a tight hold on children. You'll have to view the pretty Leavitt Falls from quite a distance, but the series of frothing cascades and pools is worth the trip. And the overlook also provides fine views of the West Walker Valley, 600 feet below.

The sites at Leavitt Meadow Campground are open May to October. No reservations. Moderate fee.

• • • • • • • • • • • • • • • • • • • • • • • •

# 28 BURST ROCK AND POWELL LAKE

Distance: 3.8 miles round trip
Difficulty: Moderate
Starting point: 8,550 feet
High point: 9,150 feet
Total climb: 880 feet
Map: USGS Pinecrest 15'

If you're looking for a primo half-day hike, with gorgeous scenery and a pretty lakeside destination, this trek to Burst Rock and Powell Lake simply can't be beat. Perhaps this hike's only drawback is its popularity, so try to visit on a weekday if at all possible.

To reach the trailhead, drive east 1.3 miles beyond the small settlement of Cold Springs on Highway 108, and turn off onto the paved Crabtree Road. Go 6.7 miles to a junction at a pack station, and continue straight onto an unpaved road, following signs for Gianelli's Cabin.

Arrive at another junction after 2.7 miles. Go straight again for Gianelli's Cabin and reach the trailhead at road's end after 4.1 miles (total of 6.8 miles on unpaved road). The ample parking area at the trailhead will clue you in to the popularity of this hike, if the hordes of backpackers' cars left behind on weekends don't.

Begin walking at a sign for the Burst Rock Trail, and descend to cross a small stream. Pass the site of historic Gianelli's Cabin on the left. Sierra historians say the cabin was built in 1905 by a man named Gianelli. Unfortunately, the rest of Gianelli's story is still a mystery.

Ascend through a forest of handsome red firs and mountain hemlocks as you continue. A steady uphill leads into a truly steep climb. This is the toughest section of the entire hike, so labor through it with your goal in mind. Arrive at a small sign for the Emigrant Wilderness at 0.4 mile, and continue up at a punishing rate.

If you find yourself staring at your feet and muttering as you struggle up the hill, watch for patches of lovely spreading phlox instead. Gain widening vistas and a more mellow incline at 0.6 mile as you finally reach the ridgetop. Continue along the ridge and veer left off the trail to walk out to the rocky knoll known as Burst Rock at 0.8 mile.

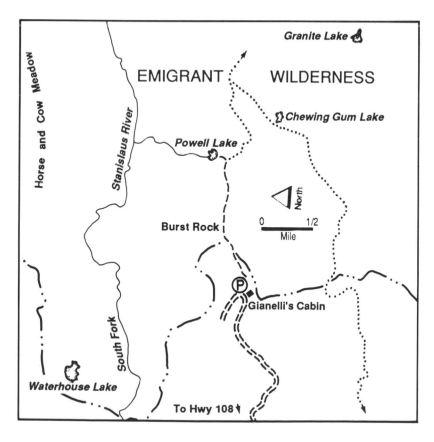

*The vista from Burst Rock includes Castle Rock, the Three Chimneys, and The Dardanelles.*

According to popular legend, a pioneer woman gave birth to her child on this rugged but scenic ridge in the latter half of the nineteenth century, en route to the promised land farther west. First known as "Birth Rock," the ridge's name evolved into the present-day Burst Rock through popular usage.

There is a fantastic view of the Old Emigrant Trail from this landmark. Horse and Cow Meadow (Hike 30) is just below, and beyond are Castle Rock, the Three Chimneys, and The Dardanelles. Linger awhile, if the often chilly wind allows, then return to the trail and savor delightful views to the south as you continue along the ridgetop. On a clear day, the vista extends as far as Mount Lyell in Yosemite National Park.

Look for pussypaws, spreading phlox, and Sierra wallflower as you begin descending at 1.1 miles. After a small pothole lake, enjoy more level walking along the ridge through a granitic landscape sprinkled with mountain hemlocks.

Wind into a thicker stand of mountain hemlocks, then watch for an unmarked trail junction at 1.8 miles (if you reach a steep uphill, you've gone too far). Veer left at the junction to make the short descent to the shore of Powell Lake at 1.9 miles. A postcard-perfect scene unfolds as you approach this enchanting little alpine lake, encircled by glowing granite slopes.

The lake is preceded by a pristine meadowy shore, so be sure to keep to established paths as you draw near the water. Pause for a picnic and some wildflower watching before backtracking along Burst Rock's ridgeline.

• • • • • • • • • • • • • • • • • • • • • • • • • •

# 29 WATERHOUSE LAKE

Distance: 3.4 miles round trip
Difficulty: Moderate
Starting point: 8,180 feet
High point: 8,180 feet
Total climb: 730 feet
Map: USGS Pinecrest 7.5'

Although this is a relatively short hike, it's a challenging one. The 0.4-mile descent to Waterhouse Lake is precipitous and tiring, and requires both routefinding and scrambling skills to negotiate the sides of the spectacular granite canyon that holds the lake. This isn't a good hike for families with young children, but it's a wonderful trek for anyone who wants an inside look at the harsh and rugged beauty of the Emigrant Wilderness.

Turn off Highway 108 2.3 miles east of Strawberry, and follow Herring Creek Road toward Herring Creek Reservoir. Drive 4.5 miles on paved road, then another 2.5 miles to a junction for the reservoir. Go right here and stay on the upper road (to the right).

Stay with the main road for 2.7 miles, then turn right onto Road 5N31 and drive another 0.7 mile (keeping left at a final junction) to reach the signposted Waterhouse Lake Trail. There's ample parking at the trailhead.

Follow the level trail onto an old roadbed crossing an open meadow. Corn lily, Brewer's lupine, nude buckwheat, and yampah decorate the ground. Begin descending gently through lodgepole pines and red firs. The old road is replaced by a narrow footpath at 0.3 mile.

Leave the meadow and descend through trees, then come in beside a second meadow where broadleaf lupine and primrose monkeyflower add splashes of blue and yellow to the green. Cross a small stream at 0.6 mile, and enjoy level walking on the flower-lined trail.

Reach a sign marking the boundary of the Emigrant Wilderness at 0.9 mile. Stark granite slopes dotted with the glacial erratics characteristic of the Sierra are ahead. Pinemat manzanita sprouts from the fissures between the stones. Continue on to gain a fine vista of the deep granite canyon cut by the South Fork of the Stanislaus River.

This is where the trail gets tricky. Because there's no topsoil to hold a beaten footpath, trail builders have left splotches of yellow paint on the rocks as a guide. Small piles of stones (ducks) also perch along the route, but it's best to rely on the painted rocks.

Begin a rough descent down the hillside, angling slightly to the left. Manzanita and canyon live oak are the brushy companions that will slow your progress. Be resigned to pokey hiking, and pause occasionally to marvel at the spectacular granite landscape. If the sun's too hot, claim a patch of shade beneath one of the tenacious Sierra junipers that spring miraculously from narrow clefts between the stones.

After 1.3 miles, the ducks and yellow paint diverge. An old streambed cutting straight downhill will alert you to the spot. The tiny ducks lead across the hillside to a lovely viewpoint just above Waterhouse Lake and an almost vertical descent route to the lakeshore from that point.

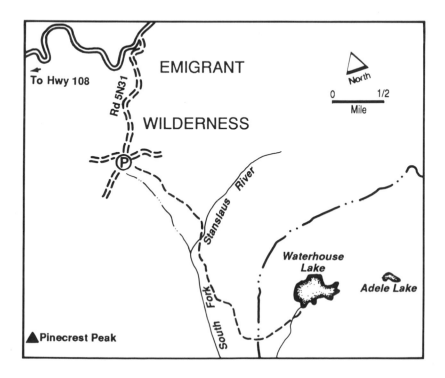

*A lone Jeffrey pine finds life in the granite above Waterhouse Lake.*

The splotches of yellow paint trace the easiest descent. They follow the path of the dry creekbed down the hill instead. It's still a steep haul, but it's better than the cliff. Descend with the paint and angle left to reach Waterhouse Lake at 1.7 miles.

Cradled in its bed of granite, Waterhouse Lake is large and deep enough for swimming. It offers flat slabs of sun-warmed rock that are perfect for sunbathing, lots of campspots for overnight visitors, and a truly remarkable setting.

# 30 HORSE AND COW MEADOW

Distance: 5.6 miles round trip
Difficulty: Easy
Starting point: 8,500 feet
High point: 8,800 feet
Map: USGS Pinecrest 15'

This is a nice hike for a family outing; you can go as long or as short a distance as you like. If you're not wild about walking a trail that's popular with horse packers, you might want to schedule

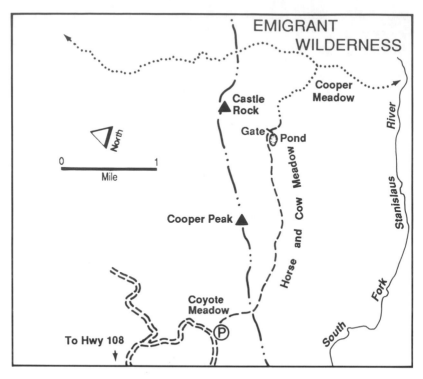

your visit for a quiet summer weekday to avoid the crowds. The flat trail is wide and easy to follow, and the wildflowers that line the way are a blossom lover's delight.

Turn off Highway 108 2.3 miles east of Strawberry, and follow Herring Creek Road toward Herring Creek Reservoir. Drive 4.5 miles on paved road, then another 2.5 miles to a junction for the reservoir. Go right here and stay on the upper road (to the right).

Stay with the main road for 4.5 miles, then turn right onto an unmarked spur road (11.5 miles from Highway 108) and drive 1.0 mile. Go left at the sign for Horse and Cow Meadow. There's parking just beyond.

A sign for the Emigrant Wilderness marks the trailhead. Begin walking through a meadow bright with broadleaf lupine, ranger buttons, fireweed, and yampah. Climb gently to enter a forest of red firs and lodgepole pines, and reach the crest of your ascent at 0.4 mile. Descend slightly, then gain level walking once again.

Pass a boundary sign for the Emigrant Wilderness at 0.6 mile. Cross a fenceline soon afterward, and begin catching glimpses of the long granite ridgeline on the right as you wind through a thin forest of firs and pines. Scarlet gilia, mule ears, and mountain pennyroyal decorate the dry earth beneath the trees.

Climb gently to reach a second crest at 1.0 mile, and turn your attention to the basalt ridgeline on the left. Carved by time and weather, it boasts surreal shapes and haunting shadows.

Continue on to enter a vast meadowland of marshy ponds and abundant wildflowers. You'll have wonderful views of the basalt ridgeline to the left, framed by the blossoms of cow parsnip and broadleaf lupine. At the 1.8-mile point, the basalt bastion of Castle Rock will claim your attention (watch for it straight ahead, across a long expanse of meadow).

Resume level walking, traipsing through bright wildflowers where the ground is damp and gaining sage and occasional lodgepole pines in the drier sections. Arrive at a small reed-lined pond at 2.6 miles. This area may be very soggy if you visit early in the season. Pass through an old dilapidated gate.

If you're ready for an end to your meadow wandering, walk about 0.2 mile past the pond and watch for a small granite outcropping to the left of the trail (just as you start downhill). Leave the path and scramble to the top of the outcropping for a view down to Cooper Meadow (east) and out toward Castle Rock (north).

For a longer hike, follow the trail as it continues down to Cooper Meadow from this point.

. . . . . . . . . . . . . . . . . . . . . . . . . . .

# 31 SWORD LAKE

Distance: 5.8 miles round trip
Difficulty: Moderate
Starting point: 7,190 feet
High point: 7,550 feet
Total climb: 1,200 feet
Map: USGS Spicer Meadows Res. 7.5'

This trail is a bit more challenging than the stroll to Boulder Creek (Hike 32), but it offers some charming scenery on the way to a pleasant alpine lake. If at all possible, try this trail on a weekday, as it's quite popular and often attracts large weekend crowds.

Turn off Highway 108 at the sign for Clark Fork (about 19 miles east of the Summit Ranger Station), and drive 0.9 mile on the paved Clark Fork Road. Just past the bridge over the Middle Fork of the Stanislaus River, turn left at a sign for Fence Creek Campground. Drive 6.3 miles on an unpaved road to the trailhead at road's end.

Actually, there are two trailheads here. The trail to the right, McCormick Creek, leads to the southeast side of The Dardanelles.

*Glacial castaways dot the granite-dominated landscape around Sword Lake.*

Start out on the County Line Trail straight ahead.

Climb gently on the dirt footpath, keeping to the main route as spur trails wander off to the side. Ascend through white firs and nude buckwheat, fighting the pull of gravity as the incline increases. Climb steadily to reach a viewpoint at 0.4 mile. You'll get a good look down onto Donnell Reservoir from here.

The trail levels out as you continue, sharing the shade of firs and pines with mule ears and mountain pennyroyal. Reach a barbed-wire fence at 0.7 mile, and continue out across an open field to arrive at a junction with the Dardanelles Spur Trail. You'll see the rugged silhouette of The Dardanelles above you on the right.

Go straight for Sword Lake. Corn lilies cover the open ground as you walk. A vista opens to the north and northwest as you descend across an open slope with broadleaf lupine, sage, yarrow, and spearmint. Reenter a forest of Jeffrey pines and red and white firs, and continue descending on the shaded trail.

Reach a small creek at 1.5 miles. The moist earth along its banks supports thimbleberries, bracken ferns, and pinedrops. Continue to a junction with the Dardanelles Creek Trail at 2.1 miles, and go right, following signs for Sword Lake. Enjoy level walking through trees, and reach a junction for Gabbott Meadow at 2.4 miles.

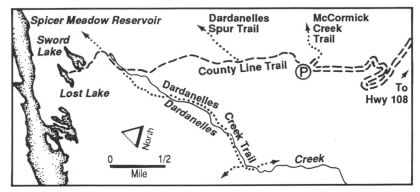

Continue to the left for Sword Lake and arrive at your destination after another 0.2 mile. Sword Lake is pleasingly picturesque, with steep granite shores and a striking blue tint. You'll spot Bull Run Peak to the north, across the water. The lake is large and deep enough for swimming.

If Sword Lake is too crowded, continue on to Lost Lake, 0.3 mile farther. To reach Lost Lake, skirt to the left along Sword Lake's fern-lined shore. There isn't a well-defined trail between these close neighbors, but you should be able to find the way without difficulty.

Lost Lake is smaller and narrower that Sword Lake, but it boasts a striking granite shoreline, and the surrounding rock shelves are littered with glacial erratics. From the crest of the rocky hillside on Lost Lake's west shore, you'll gain a view of the new Spicer Meadow Reservoir.

● ● ● ● ● ● ● ● ● ● ● ● ● ●

# 32 BOULDER CREEK

Distance: 5.3 miles round trip
Difficulty: Moderate
Starting point: 6,470 feet
High point: 6,950 feet
Map: USGS Disaster Peak 7.5'

*Taking a break on the hike to Boulder Creek*

This relaxing trek along the Clark Fork of the Stanislaus River makes a great family excursion, easily reached from the campgrounds in the area. The lower elevation of the trail ensures it'll be open earlier than other Sonora Pass hikes, and the moderate grade and good condition of the route makes it ideal for less accomplished walkers.

Turn off Highway 108 at the sign for Clark Fork (about 19.0 miles east of the Summit Ranger Station), and drive 9.0 miles on the paved Clark Fork Road. The Clark Fork Trail begins where the road ends.

Cross a small creek and enter the Carson–Iceberg Wilderness as you begin your walk. To the left, the fence-enclosed Iceberg Meadow is knee-high in wildflowers. Above the lush grass, the imposing rock face of Iceberg Peak rules a rugged wilderness.

Continue on in the shade of white firs, lodgepole and Jeffrey pines, and occasional Fremont cottonwoods as you leave the meadow's edge. Climb gently to cross a second tiny waterway, then begin a series of switchbacks at 0.3 mile. Negotiate a boulder-strewn hillside where scattered Sierra junipers sink their roots into the dry, rocky ground. Manzanita and canyon live oak compete for spots of soil.

Ascend for 0.1 mile and gain fine views of Iceberg Peak as you near the top. Enjoy a brief downhill, then move on to level walking above the Clark Fork of the Stanislaus River. This is a pretty waterway with a lot of big boulders and inviting pools for swimming. No doubt you'll be tempted to dawdle if the day is hot.

Follow the level trail beside the water, enjoying the company of Sierra alders, Fremont cottonwoods, and quaking aspens. Lush bracken ferns give testimony to the increased moisture level in the soil. Resume climbing at 0.9 mile, and labor up a rocky slope that's lovely with cone flowers, woolly mullein, and narrow goldenrod.

Enter the shade of a white fir forest once again, and watch for nude buckwheat and delicate gayophytum on the forest floor. Climb gently and cross a tributary creek at 1.5 miles. Fistfuls of ranger buttons polka-dot the banks with balls of white.

Continue up at a mellow incline. The massive trunks of long-dead trees sprawl across the shaded forest floor, looking like the

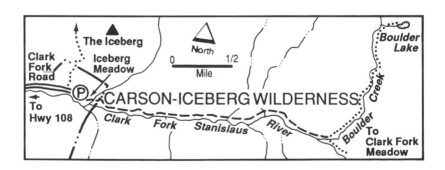

whitened bones of ancient dinosaurs. Rejoin the Clark Fork at 2.0 miles.

If you're looking for an early end to the day or an ideal picnic spot, this is the place to stop. A sandy shoreline beckons boot-weary toes to wiggle in the current, and quiet pools of water provide perfect play areas for splashing children. Unpack your lunch and linger.

If you decide to continue on to Boulder Creek, stay with the trail as it draws away from the water once again. Hike beneath white firs and Jeffrey pines. Sulfur flower, nude buckwheat, and scarlet gilia brighten the open, dusty ground.

Begin climbing more steeply at 2.4 miles, and reach Boulder Creek and the junction for Clark Fork Meadow after 0.2 mile. Straight ahead, the trail continues uphill for the small, shallow Boulder Lake, 1.5 miles farther on (the other trail continues to the right). If you have the time and energy, make the lake your destination. But be forewarned, most of your climbing is still ahead.

To regain the trailhead, retrace your steps along the dancing Clark Fork and enjoy an easy, downhill walk.

• • • • • • • • • • • • • • • • • • • • • • • • • • •

# 33   GIANT JEFFREY WALK

Distance: 2.3 miles round trip
Difficulty: Easy
Starting point: 6,080 feet
High point: 6,160 feet
Map: USGS Dardanelle 7.5'

This short, easy jaunt from Highway 108 offers a great afternoon excursion for a family suffering from campground fever or car claustrophobia. Bring along a wildflower book and pause to look up blossoms, wriggle your toes in the Middle Fork of the Stanislaus, or plunk a fishing line into its current. And pay your respects to a forest giant that almost didn't escape an untimely death by chainsaw.

Drive 3.4 miles east of Dardanelle on Highway 108, and park just west of the Douglas Picnic Area. There's ample parking beside a bridge across the Middle Fork of the Stanislaus River. The bridge was built as part of the timber sale and logging operation that almost resulted in the giant Jeffrey pine's demise. But before the loggers went to work, foresters submitted the dimensions of the tree to the American Forestry Association, and the massive Jeffrey

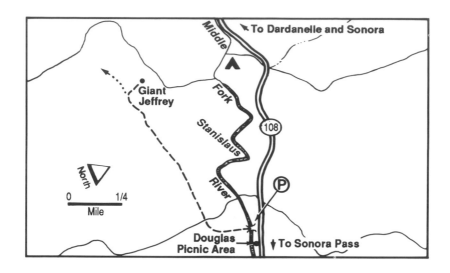

was proclaimed world champion. That saved the tree from the chainsaw blade, and a goshawk nest stalled the logging project, so the woods are quiet here, at least temporarily.

Cross the bridge and walk along an unpaved logging road that angles to the right. Mule ears and narrow goldenrod line the roadside as you climb gently beneath white firs and lodgepole and Jeffrey pines. Stay with the logging road for 1.0 mile, and watch for the aftermath of a winter avalanche. You'll see large boulders strewn across the hillside on both sides of the road.

Roughly 200 yards past the first signs of the rockslide, look for a faint footpath angling off to the right through a sage-dotted clearing. If you have trouble spotting the path, scan the skyline to the right for a tall Jeffrey pine with a forked top (about 100 yards off the road).

Head down into the meadow and merge with a more defined path. Angle left on the trail to reach the giant Jeffrey. There's a small sign at the base of the tree proclaiming it to be the World's Largest Jeffrey Pine. The dimensions listed on the sign are 96 inches DBH (diameter at breast height), 197-foot height, and 90.5-foot crown spread.

It's a magnificent specimen, with deeply furrowed bark and majestic spreading branches. Press your nose against the trunk and inhale deeply to catch the Jeffrey's characteristic butterscotch odor. If you look closely at the tree, you might see traces of the blue line around the base that once earmarked this giant for destruction. Pause awhile to enjoy the Jeffrey's shade before turning back.

# 34 RELIEF RESERVOIR VIEWPOINT

Distance: 5.6 miles round trip
Difficulty: Moderate
Starting point: 6,320 feet
High point: 7,200 feet
Map: USGS Sonora Pass 7.5'

If at all possible, try this popular hike to Relief Reservoir on a weekday. Summer weekends bring crowds of people and hordes of horses to the trail, rendering the walk less than idyllic and dulling the glow of the "wilderness experience." This is a nice hike for families with children, because the grade is moderate and the trail is good. If you want to lengthen the walk a bit, descend to Relief Reservoir from the viewpoint stopping place. Just remember, "Whoever goes down must come up."

Take the Kennedy Meadow turnoff from Highway 108, 5.5 miles southeast of Dardanelle. Drive in 1.1 miles on the paved secondary road. Pass a trailhead parking lot at 0.5 mile, but you don't have to use it if you're not staying overnight. Continue on past the Kennedy Meadow lodge and store, and reach the end of the road and limited trailhead parking.

Begin walking at a sign for the Huckleberry Trail, climbing gently on a wide dirt road. Weekends bring a score of horses, dust, and manure to this heavily used entry route into the Emigrant Wilderness, so be forewarned. Walk in the shade of incense cedars, Jeffrey pines, and white firs as you hike beside the Middle Fork of the Stanislaus River. Undoubtedly, you'll share the way with a lot of fishermen.

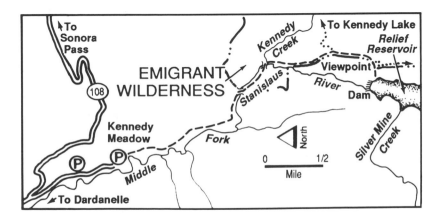

*Herds of backpackers and horses make the trail to Relief Reservoir a weekend superhighway.*

The trail levels as you skirt along the edge of the broad Kennedy Meadow. Manzanita and sage line the path and narrow goldenrod paints the ground with joyous yellows. Reach a sign marking the boundary of the Emigrant Wilderness at 1.1 miles and resume the climb from here.

You'll cross the river on a sturdy footbridge at 1.3 miles. The canyon narrows and becomes increasingly picturesque as you continue climbing. The trail is a rocky path cut into the cliffs. Tumultuous Kennedy Creek joins from the left at 1.6 miles, pouring down a chute of solid stone.

Keep climbing steadily beneath Sierra junipers and sharp-edged cliffs, then recross the Stanislaus on a high, wooden bridge, which offers a fine view down into the river channel. Canyon live oak, sage, and blue elderberry bushes line the trail as the ascent resumes.

Turn away from the river and begin a dusty trek past stampedes of mule ears, arriving at a junction for Kennedy Lake at 2.3 miles. The trail leading to the left ascends gently beside Kennedy Creek, but the distance in to the first lake rules out a manageable day hike.

Continue straight toward Relief Reservoir. After another 0.5 mile, reach an unsigned junction where a smaller trail veers off to the right. Take this short footpath to a fine viewpoint above the dam and reservoir at the 2.8-mile point.

It's a steep 0.3-mile descent to the surface of the reservoir from here. If you're carrying a fishing pole, it might be worth the trip. Otherwise, settle in to enjoy the view and a picnic lunch from your lofty perch above the water.

• • • • • • • • • • • • • • • • • • • • • • • • •

# 35 BLUE CANYON

Distance: 3.6 miles round trip
Difficulty: Strenuous
Starting point: 8,820 feet
High point: 10,040 feet
Map: USGS Sonora Pass 7.5'

For a little-known hike with unmatched alpine scenery, try this ascent up Blue Canyon. Go equipped with sturdy shoes and leave the little ones behind, as this scramble beside Blue Canyon Creek promises rough going and a few tricky sections. And be sure to time your visit for mid- to late August, as snow renders the canyon nearly impassable any earlier.

To reach the unsigned trailhead for Blue Canyon, drive 2.7 miles west of the Sonora Pass Summit on Highway 108. Watch for the 9,000-foot elevation sign, and park on the shoulder of the road just beyond it. You may want to jam a few rocks against your tires, as the grade is steep here.

Descend from the south side of Highway 108 and cross the tumbling Deadman Creek. Climb steeply on the unmarked trail beyond. Pass a signboard for the Emigrant Wilderness and continue up. The rocky trail is sometimes difficult to follow; be observant as you climb.

Ascend through scatterings of lodgepole and whitebark pines. Mule ears, nude buckwheat, and mountain pennyroyal crowd beside the trail. Inhale deeply to catch the scent of wild spearmint as you pass.

The punishing grade eases briefly at 0.3 mile. Blue Canyon Creek is on the right, awash in tower larkspur and Indian paintbrush. Cross a tributary creek and continue steeply up. When the incline takes your breath away, pause to marvel at the assortment of wildflowers that makes this hike so memorable. Sierra arnica and tall mountain helenium decorate the canyon with blazing yellow banners. Mountain sorrel hides among the rocks, and crimson columbine dangles delicate blossoms above the water.

Blue Canyon Creek descends at a breakneck incline down the narrow canyon, and waterfalls dance across the stones, adding to the splendor. Arrive at a particularly steep section of the trail at 0.8 mile. Be careful here, as the loose rocks are slippery. At this point in your climb, you may begin to wonder if this hike goes anywhere other than straight up. The truth is, it doesn't, but the scenery is worth the effort.

Cross another tributary creek at 1.0 mile, and continue up

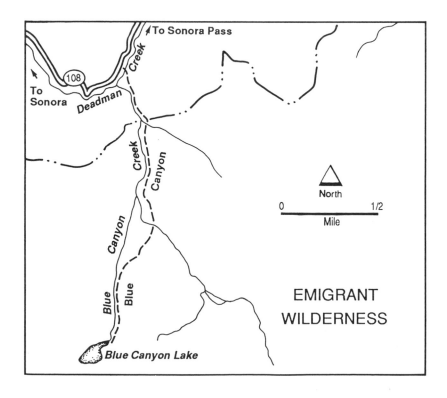

*Exquisite Blue Canyon promises an excruciating climb.*

beside Blue Canyon's churning waters. Enter a broad sloping meadow that's an avalanche of flowers. To the northeast is a view of Saint Marys Pass and Sonora Peak (Hike 36). Tall mountain helenium splashes broad swathes of yellow across the slopes, and the facing mountain headwall is awesome in its ruggedness.

Continue climbing steadily, and stick to the lower trail beside the creek as you enter a narrow, cliffy section of the creekbed. Cross the water for a brief stint on the other shore, then recross and ascend some more. If you look closely at the rocks through here, you'll see how Blue Canyon got its name. They have a definite bluish tint.

Cross a delicate carpet of alpine monkeyflower and pussypaws as you near your destination. Arrive at Blue Canyon Lake at 1.8 miles. It's a beautiful little pocket of water, tucked into the mountainside at 10,040 feet. The grassy shores are scattered with cinquefoil, primrose monkeyflower, and Brewer's lupine, and the lake's surface is as blue and still as a turquoise stone, except when the breeze ruffles its composure.

The water is icy and the lake's a bit too shallow for good swimming. But as you sit and marvel at the beauty of your surroundings, you'll feel you've climbed right into heaven's basement.

To regain Highway 108 and your starting point, retrace your route beside Blue Canyon Creek. Be sure to watch your step, as the footing is even trickier on the downhill journey.

- - - - - - - - - - - -
## 36 SAINT MARYS PASS AND SONORA PEAK

Distance: 4.6 miles round trip
Difficulty: Strenuous
Starting point: 9,430 feet
High point: 11,460 feet
Map: USGS Sonora Pass 7.5'

*Sturdy alpine buckwheat*

Where else but in the high Sierra can a hiker ascend an 11,460-foot mountain and still be back at camp in time for an early dinner? Of course, this trek to the summit of Sonora Peak begins at an elevation of 9,430 feet, but even with the lofty starting point, it's a steep haul to the top. Carry a lunch, plenty of water, and a jacket,

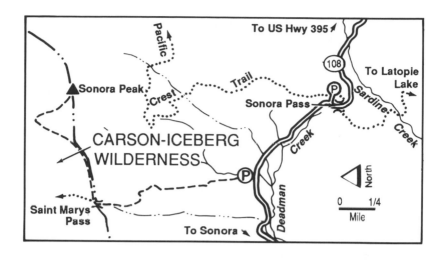

and start early in the day if there's a hint of cloud cover.

As with the Sonora Pass hike (Hike 37), midsummer snows will dictate this trail's open season. In an average snow year, you probably won't get in until August.

The trail takes off 0.8 mile west of the Sonora Pass Summit, on the north side of Highway 108. Watch for a road sign proclaiming St. Marys Pass Trailhead. You can park on the shoulder of Highway 108 or take the short (but very rough) road to an unpaved parking area.

Pass a boundary sign for the Carson–Iceberg Wilderness as you begin a steady climb through lodgepole pines and sage. Brewer's lupine, tall mountain helenium, mountain pennyroyal, and California corn lily provide a colorful preview of the abundance of wildflowers ahead. The grade increases as the trail ascends an open hillside alive with mule ears, Drummond's thistle, Indian paintbrush, and scarlet gilia.

Scrubby whitebark pines take over for the lodgepoles as you gain elevation. Struggle up the steady, steep grade, and reach a saddle at 1.2 miles. At an elevation of 10,400 feet, Saint Marys Pass offers a wide-ranging view to the north and south. Look for the silhouette of The Dardanelles to the northwest.

This pass owns a place in the history of the Sierra Nevada. It was part of the first pioneer trail across this section of the mountains, and it led to the Clark Fork of the Stanislaus River. First opened to pack animals in 1862, the route was soon eclipsed in importance by a new wagon road along Deadman Creek, the current route of Highway 108.

From Saint Marys Pass, the route to the summit of Sonora Peak is primarily a cross-country scramble. The climb is a popular one, so a sharp-eyed hiker should be able to spot traces of a footpath through the rocky terrain. From the pass, leave the main trail, turn right and follow the ridgeline upward.

The grade is steep and the terrain is rough, but that's no hardship here, as you'll be walking on a spectacular carpet of wildflowers. Watch for Layne's monkeyflower, Brewer's lupine, alpine buckwheat, and sulfur flower as you climb. Reach the top of the first knoll, descend slightly, then climb across a broad expanse of loose rock as you continue toward the summit of Sonora Peak.

The final slope is nearly vertical. You'll hit the steepest part with 1.8 miles behind you. The best route of attack is to angle left to reach the ridgeline just above, then follow it to the right toward the summit. It's a steep pitch up the ridge to reach the top, but the footing is secure enough for the faint-hearted.

Attain the summit of Sonora Peak after 2.3 miles, and gulp in the thin mountain air as you stand 11,460 feet above sea level. There is a thrilling 360-degree vista to invigorate your weary muscles. On a clear day, the view stretches all the way to Mount Lyell in the south and far north into the Carson–Iceberg Wilderness.

If you brought along a jacket and a lunch, you should be able to linger awhile on the wind-whipped summit. Take time to read a few of the notes left behind by proud mountain climbers. In 1988, a note was tacked to a wooden post atop Sonora Peak: Stanley Harrison of Citrus Heights, California, proclaimed his accomplishment in bold letters—"Climbed Sonora Peak August, 1988, at age 71."

• • • • • • • • • • • • • • • • • • • • • • •

# 37  SONORA PASS TRAILHEAD

Distance: 8.8 miles round trip
Difficulty: Strenuous
Starting point: 9,620 feet
High point: 10,840 feet
Total climb: 1,540 feet
Map: USGS Sonora Pass 7.5'

If you visit Sonora Pass in mid- to late August, this is a hike you certainly won't want to miss. Unless you're an accomplished snowfield hiker, wait for the winter snows to retreat, as the trail skirts along steep hillsides that are treacherous when snow is present. Because of the precarious footing, children shouldn't make this trek without close supervision. Bring a jacket for the ridgetop,

*The trail that leads south from Sonora Pass provides a 10,800-foot-high vista.*

as it's often cool and windy, even in late summer.

Watch for a sign just west of the Sonora Pass Summit calling out the Sonora Pass Trailhead. There's ample parking available here as well as garbage cans and toilet facilities. It's a 0.2-mile walk back along Highway 108 to reach the trail's start on the south side of the road. You'll be following a portion of the Pacific Crest Trail as you leave Highway 108 and begin to climb.

Ascend steadily for 0.1 mile. The hillsides are ablaze with Brewer's lupine, broadleaf lupine, blue flax, and mountain pennyroyal. Lodgepole and whitebark pines add their imprint to the alpine landscape as you leave the road behind. Descend to cross an open draw where mule ears, alpine buckwheat, tall mountain helenium, and Sierra arnica give testimony to the high elevation.

Gain more level walking for a time, and cross a stream awash in alpine monkeyflower at 0.7 mile. Resume climbing on a trail edged with yarrow, pussypaws, and Brewer's lupine. The views expand as you climb steadily, traversing a broad, open hillside that

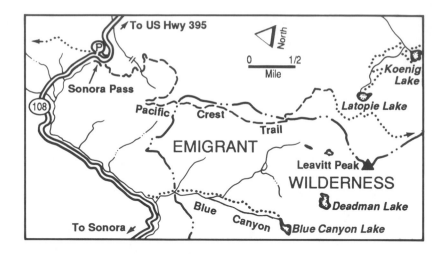

offers a fine vista of Sonora Peak (Hike 36) to the north.

Despite the challenging grade, this hike offers spectacular wildflowers and invigorating far-ranging views. Watch for meadow penstemon on the rocky slopes, and keep an eye out for the unique little plants known as Whitney's locoweed. You'll know them by their balloonlike seed pods. Brilliant eruptions of yellow monkeyflowers mark the path of tiny springs on the steep slopes.

Bushlike whitebark pines squat along the trail as you approach the ridgetop at 2.5 miles. Revel in the easy walking as you turn to angle south along the hillside. The view of endless mountains in all directions confirms that this section of the Pacific Crest Trail was aptly chosen. Reach a second saddle at 2.9 miles, and gain a widening vista to the south and east.

Continue level walking on flower-bedecked slopes. Davidson's penstemon, rockfringe, and the brilliant yellow blossoms of alpine gold (found only above 10,000 feet) will capture your attention. Watch for Deadman Lake dead ahead as you continue, then reach a saddle at 3.7 miles. From here, you'll have a view to the east of Sardine Meadow (Hike 38) and the distant Highway 108.

Begin a gentle descent as you skirt across the hillside. Be particularly careful if there's still snow on the slope. A final steep ascent will take you to your destination—a windswept saddle that offers a 10,800-foot-high view down onto a handful of alpine lakes. Latopie Lake is the closest, followed by Koenig Lake and Leavitt Lake. If you search carefully, you'll probably spot a few backpackers exploring the lakes' shorelines.

Far to the south, Tower Peak and a host of snow-capped mountains pierce the summer sky, and the jagged horizon is somewhere beyond Yosemite. Snuggle into the shelter of the rocks and picnic while you feast on the matchless beauty of this Sierra scenery.

• • • • • • • • • • • • • • • • • • • • • • • •

# 38   SARDINE FALLS

Distance: 2.0 miles round trip
Difficulty: Easy
Starting point: 8,800 feet
High point: 9,200 feet
Maps: USGS Sonora Pass 7.5′ and USGS Pickel Meadow 7.5′

This is a wonderful walk for families with young children, as the distance is short and the terrain is relatively level. And because of its proximity to Highway 108, Sardine Falls is a great excuse for a respite from the road, complete with midday picnic.

Access to this hike can be gained from Highway 108, 2.7 miles east of Sonora Pass Summit or 12.4 miles west of Highway 395. There is no off-road parking, so pull off onto the shoulder when you spot Sardine Meadow. If you're coming from Highway 395, park near the third closed road heading off into the meadow (just before Highway 108 begins to climb again).

There is no single, well-defined trail striking off into the meadow. Choose the overgrown road nearest your parking spot, and head across the grass toward the distant Sardine Falls. Watch for the bright blue blossoms of hikers gentian nestled into the lush floor of the meadow. Yarrow and wild iris add to the color scheme in July.

Cross a small creek lined with primrose monkeyflower, and continue across the meadow toward the falls. Walk through scattered lodgepole pines, climbing gently past a host of meadow wildflowers. Brewer's lupine, broadleaf lupine, scarlet gilia, and

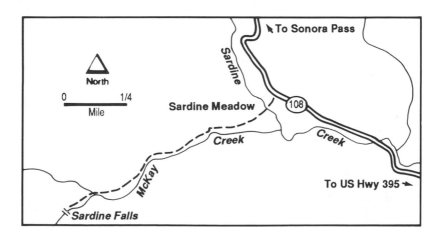

cinquefoil will clamor for your attention as you continue.

Make a short, steep ascent of a low ridge ruled by mountain pennyroyal, sulfur flower, and spearmint, then keep right as the trail branches. Continue climbing on the west side of McKay Creek. The little waterway is nearly overwhelmed with flowers, and scores of corn lilies, ranger buttons, and fireweed fight for space along its banks.

The rumble of Sardine Falls will gain intensity as you approach the base of the waterfall at 1.0 mile. Be sure to keep a tight rein on children, as the footing can be slick. Choose a comfortable viewpoint and settle in to admire the little waterfall. A white-flecked torrent tumbles down the vertical rock face here, spreading across the dark stone like a glowing wedding veil. Below, the stream is choked with color—the yellow of Sierra arnica and common monkeyflower, the lavender of fireweed, and the deep blue of tower larkspur.

Savor the beauty of the spot while you munch your sandwiches, then amble back across the meadow to regain the road.

*The hike to Sardine Falls is an easy family jaunt.*

• • • • • • • • • • • • • • • • • • • • • •

# 39  SECRET LAKE

Distance: 7.1 miles (loop)
Difficulty: Moderate
Starting point: 7,150 feet
High point: 7,760 feet
Total climb: 1,130 feet
Map: USGS Pickel Meadow 7.5'

Access to this hike is from Leavitt Meadow Campground or from the trailhead parking lot off Highway 108. The trailhead lot is just west of the campground, 8.0 miles east of Sonora Pass Summit and 7.0 miles west of Highway 395.

Add 0.4 mile to the overall distance if you're walking from the trailhead parking lot. There are toilets and drinking water available here. From the parking lot, walk east along the shoulder of Highway 108, and leave the road to angle through the campground as you descend toward the West Walker River.

A sturdy footbridge provides a dry ford of the rushing torrent. Go right with the trail on the other side. Climb beneath Sierra junipers and Jeffrey pines, then gain more level walking through sage, scrawny mountain mahogany, and leafy mule ears. A trail junction is at 0.2 mile. The West Walker Trail takes off to the right (return route). Go left for Secret Lake.

Ascend a small ridge, then descend to a petite meadow. Climb again through fragrant sage and gain more level walking at 0.9 mile. Negotiate a sage- and mahogany-covered plateau, then climb steadily once more. The terrain levels off at 1.3 miles, and you'll be rewarded with a view to the south of jagged Tower Peak (elevation 11,755 feet). Below and to the right, the broad green swathe of Leavitt Meadow hugs the curves of the West Walker River.

Traverse a juniper-studded ridgetop, then ascend a final rocky incline with views to the east of Kirman Lake. At 2.0 miles, the high point of your climb, pause to enjoy the vista of the southern mountains before beginning your descent. Watch for Poore Lake off to the left.

Another 0.5 mile brings you to the emerald surface of Secret Lake. Surrounded by Jeffrey pines and Sierra junipers, Secret Lake is a pretty little gem with a fine shoreline for swimming. It's the nicest lake on this hike, so if it's late in the day, spread a picnic here. Note the trail taking off to the right as you approach the shore. Continue on this path when you resume hiking.

Leave the lake and wind through a rocky landscape of pines and junipers. Traverse roller-coaster terrain for 0.5 mile before

*Quiet Roosevelt Lake is a pleasant link in the Secret Lake loop.*

reaching a junction marked for Poore Lake (left) and Roosevelt Lake (straight). Continue straight for Roosevelt Lake and reach a second junction soon after. If desired, a cutoff trail signed "Campground/pack station" will decrease the loop by 1.6 miles.

Otherwise, continue straight for Roosevelt Lake, noting the sudden abundance of horse manure as you merge with the packers' trail. Descend gently beneath quaking aspens and reach Roosevelt Lake at 3.6 miles. The lake's mirror-like surface reflects an open shoreline of grass and pines. Continue right along the shore to reach nearby Lane Lake. Woolly mullein, wild iris, and lupine line the way.

Lane Lake is murky and shallow, an uninviting backwater connected to Roosevelt Lake by a broad channel of water. Backpackers can continue on from here toward Fremont Lake and Chain of Lakes. To begin the return route toward Leavitt Meadow Campground, retrace your steps for 0.8 mile to reach the junction signed for "Campground/pack station." Go left toward the campground.

Walk through a watery draw of Fremont cottonwoods, willows,

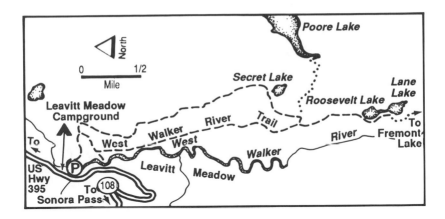

and quaking aspens, then begin a gentle descent toward Leavitt Meadow. Reach an unsigned trail junction and keep right, skirting along a dusty hillside with views down into the meadow. In an effort to preserve the easily damaged grasslands of the meadow, Forest Service personnel have rerouted the trail to keep hikers on the hillside. If you look closely, you'll be able to spot the old route down below.

Scarlet gilia, matilija poppies, mule ears, and narrow goldenrod brighten the trailside as you continue. Reach the valley floor at 5.4 miles, and glance over your shoulder for impressive views of Tower Peak and the surrounding mountains. Shun the turnoff for the pack station at 5.9 miles, and continue on a much-improved (and horseless) trail to reach an unsigned junction at 6.7 miles. Stay with the lower route to the left.

At 6.9 miles, reach another junction, go left to rejoin your entry route, and retrace your steps to Leavitt Meadow Campground.

# CHAPTER SIX

• • • • • • • • •

# Ebbetts Pass (Highway 4)

Ebbetts Pass is named for Major John Ebbetts, who set out in 1853 to find a route across the Sierra Nevada that would serve for the construction of an east-west railroad line. Although Ebbetts soon concluded that attempting to establish a rail line across this section of the mountains would be a futile endeavor, he did succeed in crossing the crest of the Sierra at the present-day Ebbetts Pass.

Ebbetts Pass wasn't frequented by the many emigrant parties that struggled westward during the mid-nineteenth century, but a stage road was established here in 1864 to serve the mining town of Silver City. Today Highway 4 leads west into Sierra foothills rich in gold-rush history, with towns like Murphys and Angels Camp conjuring up images of the region's colorful past.

Camping options are plentiful along Highway 4, and recreation opportunities abound. Calaveras Big Trees State Park is the major drawing card on the mountains' western flank, with scenic Lake Alpine the hot spot nearer to the summit. The new Spicer Meadow Reservoir, slated for completion in 1990, is sure to be a major tourist destination spot as well.

Wilderness areas accessed by the hikes in this section are the Carson–Iceberg Wilderness (refer to chapter 5) and the Mokelumne Wilderness. The 100,000-plus acres of the Mokelumne Wilderness are parcelled out between the Stanislaus and Eldorado national forests. Highway 4 runs along the south side of the wilderness area.

You won't need permits for day hikes off Highway 4, but overnight visitors and those in quest of maps, literature, and camping information can stop in or write to Stanislaus National Forest, Calaveras Ranger Station, PO Box 500, Hathaway Pines, California 95233. This station serves visitors approaching from the west.

If you're coming from the east, there are ranger stations in Bridgeport and Markleeville. Or write to Toiyabe National Forest, Carson Ranger District, 1536 South Carson Street, Carson City, Nevada 89701.

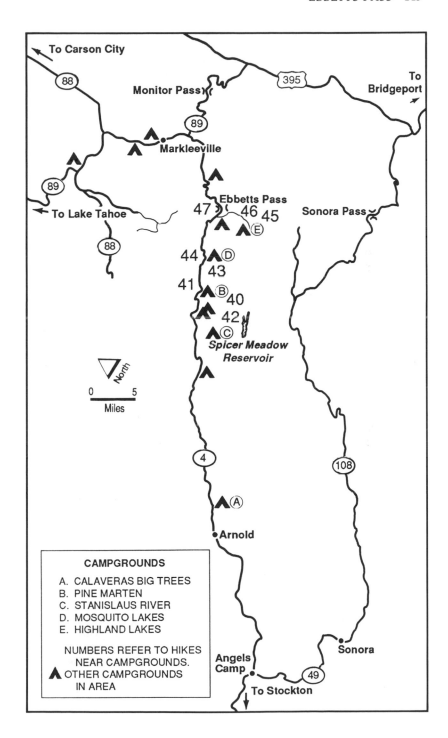

To Carson City

88

Monitor Pass

395

To Bridgeport

89

Markleeville

89

To Lake Tahoe

Ebbetts Pass

47

46 45

Sonora Pass

88

(E)

44

(D)

43

41

(B)

40

42

(C)

Spicer Meadow Reservoir

North

0 — 5
Miles

4

108

(A)

Arnold

CAMPGROUNDS

A. CALAVERAS BIG TREES
B. PINE MARTEN
C. STANISLAUS RIVER
D. MOSQUITO LAKES
E. HIGHLAND LAKES

NUMBERS REFER TO HIKES NEAR CAMPGROUNDS.
⛰ OTHER CAMPGROUNDS IN AREA

Angels Camp

Sonora

49

To Stockton

## CAMPGROUNDS

**Calaveras Big Trees State Park**   Located on the south side of Highway 4, just northeast of the settlement of Arnold, Calaveras Big Trees State Park is a stop worth making for those visiting the Ebetts Pass area. There's a lot to see here, and if you choose to linger, several reservation campgrounds are available.

Six thousand acres of pine forest and two stately groves of giant sequoias await exploration in the park, and there are several miles of hiking trails to wander. Stop at the visitor center near the entrance to pick up information on camping and hiking opportunities.

**Pine Marten Campground** *(Hike 40, Inspiration Point; Hike 41, Woodchuck Basin Trail)*   Situated on the shore of the popular Lake Alpine, Pine Marten Campground boasts more than 30 sites for tents and motorhomes, all of which are usually full on weekends. Come early if you hope to claim a place.

To find Pine Marten Campground, turn off Highway 4 onto Lake Alpine's East Shore Road (on the east end of Lake Alpine). The turnoff is just past the Chickaree Picnic Area. Follow the lakeside road and go right for Pine Marten Campground and Inspiration Point to the campground entrance.

Sites offer flush toilets, drinking water, fireplaces, and picnic tables. Some campspots have a view of the lake as well. Open June to mid-October. No reservations. Moderate fee.

**Stanislaus River Campground** *(Hike 42, Elephant Rock Lake)*   This quiet campground on the North Fork of the Stanislaus River boasts about a dozen sites for tents or motorhomes. The campspots are pleasantly shaded and the campground has a comfy feel to it. Of course, things may pick up drastically when visitors begin to flock to the new Spicer Meadow Reservoir in the next few years.

To reach the campground, drive east 1.7 miles past Big Meadow Campground on Highway 4. Turn onto the signed Spicer Reservoir Road and drive 3.0 miles on pavement before turning right into the campground. Sites offer drinking water, fireplaces, picnic tables, and non-flush toilets. Open June to October. No reservations. Moderate fee.

**Mosquito Lakes Campground** *(Hike 44, Heiser Lake; Hike 46, Noble Lake; Hike 47, Upper Kinney Lake)*   The primitive but popular Mosquito Lakes Campground is a good camping option for latecomers on a busy weekend. It's also a great access to Hike 44, Heiser Lake. Because there's no drinking water here, this tiny campground doesn't fill up as quickly as some other Ebbetts Pass facilities.

To get to Mosquito Lakes Campground, drive 5.8 miles east

of Lake Alpine's East Shore Road on Highway 4, and turn north just across from the fisherman-flooded Mosquito Lakes. A handful of tentsites offer picnic tables and fireplaces, and non-flush toilets are provided. Nights are chilly here, as the elevation is above 8,000 feet. Open June to October. No reservations. No fee.

**Highland Lakes Campground** (*Hike 45, Asa Lake*) This scenic campground is situated near the twin Highland Lakes, where fishing and deer hunting opportunities abound. To find Highland Lakes Campground, drive 12.7 miles east of Lake Alpine's East Shore Road (or 1.4 miles west of the Ebbetts Pass Summit) on Highway 4, and turn south for Highland Lakes. Drive 5.8 miles on the unpaved road to reach the spacious facility. (The rough drive in makes this a questionable destination for trailers.)

More than 20 sites offer drinking water, fireplaces, picnic tables, and non-flush toilets. Open June to October. No reservations. Moderate fee.

• • • • • • • • • • • • • • • • • • • • • • • • • •

# 40 INSPIRATION POINT

Distance: 2.2 miles round trip
Difficulty: Moderate
Starting point: 7,310 feet
High point: 7,920 feet
Map: USGS Spicer Meadows Res. 7.5'

This short but challenging hike will reward you with a delight-ful peek into the Carson–Iceberg Wilderness and down onto the popular Lake Alpine. Small children may have difficulty on the steeper sections of the climb, but a steady, slow pace should get even the casual hiker to the top. Be sure to carry a windbreaker, water, and a lunch so you can linger and enjoy a view that's truly inspirational. If you like matching names with peaks, bring a good map along as well.

The best campground access to this hike is from Pine Marten Campground, on the shore of Lake Alpine. To reach the trailhead, turn off Highway 4 onto Lake Alpine's East Shore Road (on the east end of Lake Alpine). The turnoff is just past the Chickaree Picnic Area. Follow the lakeside road and go right for Pine Marten Campground and Inspiration Point. Continue past the campground entrance and watch for the Inspiration Point/Lakeshore Trail trailhead sign just beyond. (If you reach the pack station, you've gone too far.) There's limited parking available at the trailhead.

Set out on the well-defined Lakeshore Trail, shaded by an abundance of lodgepole pines, and keep to the left as a side trail joins in from Pine Marten Campground soon afterward. You'll gain views of the expansive Lake Alpine as you continue. Merge with a trail from the pack station and pick up the inevitable scent of horse manure, then reach the junction for Inspiration Point at 0.4 mile.

Go left here and begin to climb on an exceedingly dusty trail. The grade is moderate at first, but it steepens rapidly. Cross an open, rocky slope with views down to Lake Alpine, then reenter a forest of lodgepole pines and shade-producing red firs.

A brief but agonizingly steep pitch leads out into the open once again as you reach the ridgeline at 0.8 mile. This ridge is a worthy goal in itself, providing excellent views to the south. But once you've come this far, you'll want to struggle on toward the summit.

Angle left to ascend along the ridgeline toward Inspiration Point. A couple of very steep sections with lousy footing require careful walking; use caution and take your time. For the most part, the trail is good, and you can treat yourself to wonderful vistas as you climb. Be sure to note the interesting composition of the slopes as well. You'll see a lot of lahar, the product of volcanic mudflows.

Reach the crest of the ridge at 1.1 miles. The Inspiration Point Summit is a barren, nearly flat mound, and it's often cold and windswept; the view, however, will warm you to your toes—that is, if the climb hasn't already overheated you. Wander around and

*A hiker marvels at the view from Inspiration Point.*

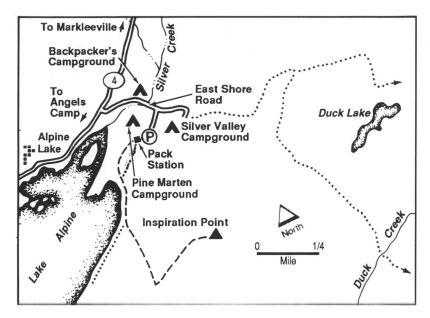

sample the vista from every angle, then pick a spot to spread a scenic picnic on.

Look for Lake Alpine, Duck Lake, Elephant Rock, and Utica and Union reservoirs, as well as the newly formed Spicer Meadow Reservoir. The Dardanelles and Dardanelles Cone are also noteworthy landmarks. When your stomach and your eyes have had their fill, turn your legs downhill.

● ● ● ● ● ● ● ● ● ● ● ● ● ● ● ● ● ● ● ● ● ● ● ●

# 41 WOODCHUCK BASIN TRAIL

Distance: 3.8 miles round trip
Difficulty: Moderate
Starting point: 7,800 feet
High point: 8,850 feet
Maps: USGS Spicer Meadows Res. 7.5' and USGS Pacific Valley 7.5'

This hike to the ridge above Wheeler Lake is a wonderful outing for those in search of a great vista without an overwhelming climb. The ascent is well graded, for the most part, and the trail is well maintained. Children should have no trouble with the ter-

*The Woodchuck Basin hike leads to a rugged ridgetop.*

rain, and wildflower lovers will be enthralled with the blossoms along the way.

To reach the trailhead, drive east 1.3 miles beyond Lake Alpine's East Shore Road on Highway 4. Turn north at a sign for the Woodchuck Basin trailhead. Drive 0.3 mile on a rough, unpaved road (you can park earlier, if the road is too primitive), and begin walking at a sign simply stating "trail."

Climb through mountain hemlocks, lodgepole pines, and red firs, ascending steadily for about half a mile. If you're a flower watcher, there are plenty of excuses to stop for breathers. Look for nude buckwheat, yarrow, and mountain pennyroyal as you begin, then pick up mule ears and Brewer's lupine a little farther on.

Get a break in the climbing at 0.5 mile, and hike across a grassy hilltop brightened with California corn lily, Sierra arnica, yampah, and death camas. Cross a small stream in the shadow of an imposing basalt ridge, then wind on beneath scattered western white pines as you work across a hillside trampled by a stampede of mule ears.

The ascent picks up again from here, with views of the vast Lake Alpine. Look for Inspiration Point (Hike 40) above the lake. You should be able to spot Elephant Rock, Utica and Union reservoirs, and The Dardanelles as well.

Climb a long, open hillside at a steady, moderate pace. The mule ears are joined by mountain pennyroyal and sulfur flower. The grade intensifies as the trail approaches a saddle in the ridge. Reach the crest of the climb and a trail junction at 1.7 miles.

Continue straight for Wheeler Lake and pass an entry sign for the Mokelumne Wilderness. Climb gently as you hike along the north side of the ridge. Mountain hemlocks and western white pines will offer you a bit of shade as you go on.

At a second saddle in the ridge at 1.8 miles, the trail plunges 1,000 feet to reach the shore of Wheeler Lake. To the left of the trail, note the large basalt outcropping painted with bright patches of lichen. To find your view and avoid the dive to Wheeler Lake

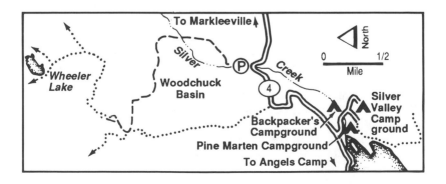

(and the inevitable climb back up), abandon the trail proper at this point.

Simply scramble up the slope to the right (there are several faint use trails) and gain the ridgetop at 1.9 miles. You'll be standing at 8,850 feet on the summit of the ridge, and the view is fantastic in all directions.

To the south, look for Lake Alpine and Inspiration Point, Utica and Union reservoirs, and the new Spicer Meadow Reservoir, as well as The Dardanelles. To the north is the rugged country traversed by Carson Pass. The large canyon in the distance is cut by the North Fork of the Mokelumne River, and you can catch a glimpse of Wheeler Lake below, shrouded by the trees. To the east, look for the rugged forms of Highland and Silver peaks. Rest your legs and feast your eyes on the rocky ridgetop carpeted with lupine, sage, and mountain pennyroyal.

## 42   ELEPHANT ROCK LAKE

Distance: 5.8 miles (loop)
Difficulty: Easy
Starting point: 6,920 feet
High point: 7,350 feet
Map: USGS Spicer Meadows Res. 7.5′

*Blazes lead the way to Rock Lake.*

This easy loop hike makes an excellent family outing. It offers pleasant forest walking, stops at three nicely spaced lakes, and the added attraction of no need for backtracking. The final 0.8 mile of the walk is along the unpaved trailhead access road, so it's possible to shorten the loop with a car shuttle for the younger or less energetic members of your hiking group.

To reach the trailhead for Elephant Rock Lake, drive east 1.7 miles past Big Meadow Campground on Highway 4. Turn onto the signed Spicer Reservoir Road and drive 8.1 miles on pavement before turning left onto the unpaved Road 7N01 (signed for Elephant Rock Lake). Continue on Road 7N01 for 4.0 miles to reach the trailhead.

Begin walking at a sign for Elephant Rock Lake (there's also a sign for Duck Lake/Rock Lake). Since portions of this trail are open to mountain bikes, keep an eye out for cyclists. Keep to the right at the first junction (with the sign for mountain bikes), and reach a second junction soon after.

Go left here to make the short side trip to petite Elephant Rock Lake. Scattered lily pads, a grassy shoreline brightened with primrose monkeyflower, and the nearby bulk of Elephant Rock make this lake a scenic treat. Because of its proximity to the road and its delicate shoreline, Elephant Rock Lake is closed to camping.

Skirt to the right along the lakeshore (or return to the junction and go left) to rejoin the trail toward Rock Lake. Walk a level, shaded path beneath lodgepole pines, red and white firs, and stout Jeffrey pines to yet another junction at 0.3 mile.

Continue straight for Rock Lake as you enter the Carson–Iceberg Wilderness. Climb gently with views of Elephant Rock to the left, then gain more level walking as the trail winds on through the forest. Like its more famous relation, The Dardanelles, Elephant Rock is composed of volcanic material left behind by ancient lava flows.

Cross several small creeks as you continue (many will be dry in late season), and skirt around a lot of fallen trees as well. Watch for ducks when the trail is indistinct. Climb gently into a granite-dominated landscape sprinkled with Jeffrey pines. The grade increases as you ascend a low ridge, then returns to a more mellow uphill through the trees.

Arrive at shallow Rock Lake at 1.9 miles. This attractive lake is aptly named, as its crystal-clear water is studded with a lot of small rock islands. If you arrive around midday, Rock Lake will make an excellent lunch spot. It's the nicest place to linger on this hike.

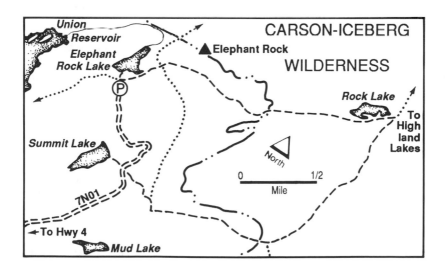

Continue with the trail to the far end of the lake, and arrive at a junction for Highland Lakes at 2.2 miles. Go right here and follow a level route through trees before starting gently downhill past lodgepole pines and a lot of manzanita. Reach another junction at 3.5 miles, and go right for Summit Lake.

Climb gradually for a time, then gain level walking once again. At 4.4 miles is a sign marking your departure from the Carson–Iceberg Wilderness. Keep to the right as the trail branches, then climb to a junction signed for Summit Lake. Go left here and cross Road 7NO1 at 4.8 miles. Continue with the trail to arrive at Summit Lake 0.1 mile later.

Although not as scenic as Elephant Rock Lake or Rock Lake, Summit Lake is large and fairly deep, with a shoreline crowded with firs and pines. Pause for a look, or linger long enough to peel off your shoes and socks and cool your toes, then backtrack to the road to begin the last leg of your walk. Go left on Road 7NO1 and regain your starting point at 5.8 miles.

# 43  BULL RUN LAKE

Distance: 7.2 miles round trip
Difficulty: Moderate
Starting point: 7,800 feet
High point: 8,350 feet
Total climb: 1,280 feet
Maps: USGS Spicer Meadows Res. 7.5' and USGS Pacific Valley 7.5'

This hike offers an enjoyable mix of downhill, level, and uphill walking; an interesting blend of meadows, forest, and granite; and a very scenic destination in Bull Run Lake. The lake is a treat for anglers, swimmers, and picnickers alike, and it's a popular destination for short backpacking trips. If you're early in the year, you'll probably leave with soggy feet, as there are several creek crossings.

To reach the trailhead, drive east 3.9 miles beyond Lake Alpine's East Shore Road on Highway 4, and turn at a sign for the Stanislaus Meadow trailhead. Drive in on a rutted, unpaved road for 0.6 mile to reach the trail's start (you may want to park earlier if your vehicle has poor clearance). There's a trail sign where the hike begins.

Start out beside the fenced Stanislaus Meadow, made green by the flowing waters of the North Fork of the Stanislaus River. You'll begin with level walking on a trail shaded by lodgepole pines

*Lovely Bull Run Lake offers tempting picnic spots.*

and mountain hemlocks, then descend gently to enter the Carson–Iceberg Wilderness at 0.6 mile.

Continue downhill through a forest of lodgepole pines and red firs, and gain more level walking at 1.0 mile. Slosh through a gully bottom watered by several seasonal streams. Your wet feet will be rewarded with the company of a lot of early wildflowers. Look for yarrow, lupine, California corn lily, and nude buckwheat.

Ascend gently as you leave the gully, climbing through mountain hemlocks and western white pines. Cross another creek at 1.6 miles, and continue uphill through a rocky draw filled with canyon live oak, pinemat manzanita, and brightly colored Indian paintbrush. The creekbed on your right harbors mountain pennyroyal and fragrant wild spearmint.

Continue climbing steadily, watching for scattered junipers clinging to the granite-sheathed earth. The trail is marked with small ducks through here. Arrive at a junction at 2.3 miles and keep right for Bull Run Lake. The trail is level for a while, but the climb resumes at 2.7 miles.

Begin the final ascent to Bull Run Lake as you labor up a granite-studded slope, tracing the route with the help of frequently placed ducks. Zigzag across a tumbling seasonal stream. A small pond offers a brief break in the ascent at 3.2 miles, then it's uphill again as you scramble a low granite ridge.

Arrive at lovely Bull Run Lake at 3.6 miles. If you're a swimmer or a sunbather, the large rock island in the middle of the lake will probably prove irresistible. With a shoreline shaded by mountain hemlocks and lodgepole pines and a scenic backdrop formed by a semicircle of granite cliffs, Bull Run Lake is definitely a spot to linger and enjoy.

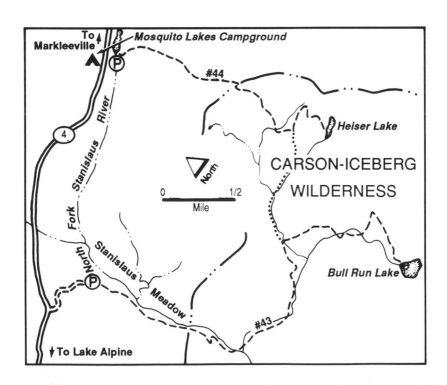

● ● ● ● ● ● ● ● ● ● ● ● ●
# 44  HEISER LAKE

Distance: 4.4 miles round trip
Difficulty: Moderate
Starting point: 8,060 feet
High point: 8,450 feet
Total climb: 1,160 feet
Maps: USGS Spicer Meadows Res. 7.5'
     and USGS Pacific Valley 7.5'

*The handsome bark of a western
white pine*

Because of its length, this little jaunt to Heiser Lake makes a fine family outing. But don't be fooled by the short 4.4-mile total distance—the roller-coaster trail to Heiser Lake will definitely satisfy your desire for some exercise! Excellent trailhead access can be obtained from the Mosquito Lakes Campground, just off Highway 4. To find the trail to Heiser Lake, drive 5.8 miles east of Lake Alpine's East Shore Road on Highway 4, and turn south at a sign for Heiser Lake Trailhead. There's limited parking here, so you'll have to compete for spots with the schools of fishermen that gather at the marshy Mosquito Lakes.

Start off on the footpath beside Mosquito Lake, and angle up the hillside with the trail behind the lake, climbing steeply beneath mountain hemlocks, lodgepole pines, and red firs. Reach the ridgetop and the end of your first ascent at 0.4 mile, then gain level walking through the trees. A gradual descent will take you to an entry sign for the Carson–Iceberg Wilderness at 0.6 mile.

Continue on a level, sometimes downhill trail through forest to reach a small pond and meadow at 0.9 mile. This spot marks the start of yet another climb. A steady ascent leads to a ridgetop at 1.1 miles. Catch a breather in the shadow of several stout western white pines, then start downhill again.

Skirt below a granite outcropping where hardy pinemat manzanita clings to the rocks. Resume climbing at 1.5 miles and arrive at a trail junction at 1.7 miles. Keep left for Heiser Lake and ascend steadily from here. The summit is about half a mile farther. A brief descent leads to the shore of Heiser Lake at 2.2 miles.

With the roller-coaster trail behind you (and all the downhills now transformed to uphills for your return), you'll want to stop awhile and sample the pleasures of pretty little Heiser Lake. Tree-lined shores and a sprinkling of tiny rock islands make this a scenic picnic spot. The lake is fairly shallow, but the water temperature is mild enough for swimming.

# 45 ASA LAKE

Distance: 4.6 miles round trip
Difficulty: Easy
Starting point: 8,480 feet
High point: 8,580 feet
Total climb: 360 feet
Maps: USGS Ebbetts Pass 7.5' and USGS Dardanelles Cone 7.5'

The walk to Asa Lake is an excellent family outing—gentle inclines, flower-filled meadows, and a pleasant destination add up to an enjoyable excursion for all ages. Pack along a lunch and a wildflower book, and plan to make a day of it.

To reach the trailhead, drive 12.7 miles east of Lake Alpine's East Shore Road (or 1.4 miles west of the Ebbetts Pass Summit) on Highway 4, and turn south for Highland Lakes. Drive 5.0 miles on the unpaved road to reach the signed Gardner Meadow trailhead. There's ample parking here. Best campground access to this hike can be gained from Highland Lakes Campground, 0.8 mile beyond the trailhead.

Begin at a sign for Upper Gardner Meadow/Wolf Creek Pass, starting out on a rocky, well-defined trail. Cross a creek edged with ranger buttons and bright-blossomed lupine, then continue on

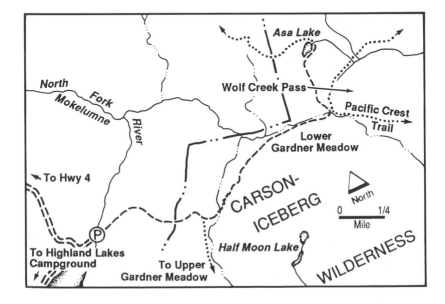

*Asa Lake's sparkling inlet stream springs right from the forest floor.*

through a wildflower-filled meadow. Look for California corn lily, yampah, Brewer's lupine, and mountain pennyroyal.

Descend to cross a seasonal creek at 0.3 mile, its banks brightened with the yellow faces of alpine monkeyflower and Sierra arnica. The trail branches soon after, as use trails split off here and there. Keep to the left and wind around the hillside to cross yet another creek.

Begin climbing from here, with scattered western white pines to offer shade. Reach an entry sign for the Carson–Iceberg Wilderness at 0.6 mile, and descend to a trail junction soon after. Continue straight for Asa Lake, cruising along the edge of a broad meadow.

Wind downhill through lodgepole pines to arrive at Lower Gardner Meadow at 1.3 miles. You'll see the effects of heavy grazing when hiking late in the season. Trampled grass and nearly nonexistent wildflowers are the cattle's calling cards.

Leave the meadow and walk beside a small stream to arrive at a signed trail junction at 1.8 miles. Two trails angle left from here. Take the first one (hard left) for Asa Lake and trace a portion of the Pacific Crest Trail as you continue.

Climb gently along a rocky hillside, passing a barbed-wire fence at 2.1 miles. Arrive at the signed turnoff for Asa Lake just after. Keep left and ascend steeply through red firs and lodgepole pines to gain the shore of petite Asa Lake at 2.2 miles.

Asa Lake is fairly shallow, but it boasts a shaded shoreline that's fine for picnicking. There are several campspots near the lake, and the place is particularly popular with bow hunters in late summer.

• • • • • • • • • • • • • • • • • • • • • •

# 46  NOBLE LAKE

Distance: 8.6 miles round trip
Difficulty: Moderate
Starting point: 8,710 feet
High point: 8,880 feet
Total climb: 1,580 feet
Map: USGS Ebbetts Pass 7.5'

This is a challenging hike with some truly sensational Sierra scenery. Be sure to wait until well into the hiking season to take it on, however, as steep slopes and lingering snowfields make the trail dangerous early in the summer.

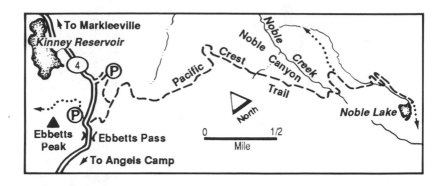

To find the trailhead for Noble Lake, drive Highway 4 to the Ebbetts Pass Summit (14.1 miles east of Lake Alpine's East Shore Road). There's roadside parking right at the summit, or you can continue 0.1 mile east and turn onto an unpaved spur road. Parking and toilets are also available 0.3 mile east of the summit.

Look for a Pacific Crest Trail sign marking the trailhead on the south side of Highway 4 (just east of the summit). Set out beneath mountain hemlocks and lodgepole and western white pines as you enjoy mostly level walking along the hillside. You'll spot California corn lily, mountain pennyroyal, and Brewer's lupine scattered beside the trail.

Merge with a trail from the main parking area at 0.3 mile, and continue gently uphill to emerge onto an open hillside at 0.5 mile. Fuzzy-leaved mule ears are abundant here, but the view is the real attraction. The vistas to the north and southeast are wonderful. With a little extra effort, an even more spectacular panorama awaits: simply scramble up the open ridge on the left side of the trail (ruled by a small rock cairn) to gain a commanding view of the surrounding peaks.

Continue with the main trail, descending slightly as you wind along the hillside. Brilliant patches of Sierra arnica and a lot of deep green mountain hemlocks make for scenic walking. Note the large chunks of volcanic lahar scattered everywhere, fallen portions of the basalt ridge above.

Cross several seasonal streams at 0.8 mile, then climb past banks of lupine as you work your way through roller-coaster terrain. A long, forested descent begins at 1.3 miles. Look for red firs, western white pines, and mountain hemlocks growing above a carpet of hardy pinemat manzanita. More open slopes boast mule ears, Indian paintbrush, sage, and scattered Sierra junipers.

You'll be treated to lovely views of Noble Canyon as you continue. Reach the first of two major creeks flowing down through the canyon at 2.8 miles. The descent ends as you tiptoe across banks overwhelmed with Sierra arnica and common monkeyflower.

*Pacific Crest Trail, Noble Lake*

Fantastic volcanic boulders make the landscape almost surreal.

Begin climbing as you skirt up and around a low ridge and ascend into Noble Canyon. Pass an unsigned secondary trail at 3.1 miles. (Note this junction, to be sure you don't take the wrong trail on the way back out.) Arrive at Noble Creek at 3.4 miles; cross it and continue climbing along a lahar-scattered hillside.

When the trail inspires you to take a breather, turn back for wonderful views of the peaks to the north of Ebbetts Pass. Negotiate a scenic, zigzagging ascent above Noble Creek. The grade is moderate but unrelenting. The vistas are nothing short of spectacular, framed by rock and sage.

Noble Lake is off to the right as you emerge onto a hilltop covered with mule ears. Take the turnoff trail that leads to the larkspur-dotted shore of Noble Lake at 4.3 miles. This is a superb picnic spot, a petite and beautiful alpine lake situated perfectly for dazzling views toward the north. The water is too cool to tempt any but the most hardy swimmer, but the surroundings are so pleasant, you'll surely want to linger.

• • • • • • • • • • • • • • • • • • • • • • • •

# 47 UPPER KINNEY LAKE

Distance: 3.8 miles round trip
Difficulty: Easy
Starting point: 8,710 feet
High point: 8,870 feet
Total climb: 590 foot
Map: USGS Ebbetts Pass 7.5′

This short, easy hike offers fine views, a lot of wildflowers, and generally pleasant walking along a portion of the lofty Pacific Crest Trail, as well as the added benefit of a neat destination lake. What more could you want in an afternoon outing?

To find the trailhead for Upper Kinney Lake, drive Highway 4 to the Ebbetts Pass Summit (14.1 miles east of Lake Alpine's East Shore Road). There's roadside parking right at the summit, or you can continue 0.1 mile east and turn onto an unpaved spur road. Parking and toilets are also available 0.3 mile east of the summit.

The trail to Upper Kinney Lake takes off on the north side of the road, 0.1 mile east of Ebbetts Pass Summit. Set out beneath mountain hemlocks and western white and lodgepole pines, with the dark basalt mound of Ebbetts Peak visible to the north. Wind through a dry alpine landscape of sage and sulfur flower as you skirt along the hillside just above Highway 4.

A short spur trail leads to an overlook with fine views of Highland and Silver peaks to the east. Make the detour, then return to the main trail and continue up beside a granite knoll studded with gnarled old Sierra junipers. The trailside is enlivened with the blossoms of mule ears, mountain pennyroyal, Brewer's lupine, and nude buckwheat.

Enjoy a stretch of level walking at 0.4 mile, and look for the jagged outlines of Reynolds and Raymond peaks to the north as you continue. Another signed overlook spot offers a peek at Kinney

Reservoir, then descend gently and pass a set of murky ponds at 0.6 mile.

Climb through a dry landscape with scattered mountain hemlocks and western white pines, then cross a seasonal creek with numerous lupine and California corn lily. You'll pass another pond at 1.2 miles. Begin a gentle descent and gain a view to the right of Lower Kinney Lake.

The descent becomes a moderate ascent as you continue, savoring a wonderful vista of rugged Raymond Peak in the distance. Climb to a junction signed for Upper and Lower Kinney Lakes at 1.7 miles and see Upper Kinney Lake below. Follow the sign for Upper Kinney Lake as you angle right to descend toward the lake, reaching the lakeshore at 1.9 miles.

Upper Kinney Lake is deep and clear, and offers a refreshing swim to the hearty and a leisurely picnic to the hungry. Peel off your shoes, plop in a fishing line, break out the sandwiches, and enjoy.

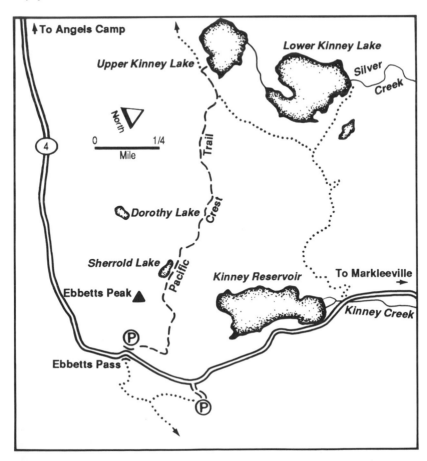

# CHAPTER SEVEN

• • • • • • • •

# Carson Pass (Highway 88)

Mountain man extraordinaire, scout, explorer, guide—all of these describe Christopher "Kit" Carson. Rugged Carson Pass is his namesake. In 1844, Carson led Captain John Fremont, the famous Sierra explorer, across the Sierra crest near the present-day Carson Pass Summit. A stunning wilderness of lakes and peaks unfolded before them as they pushed onward, and that wilderness still awaits the visitor today.

Trailheads off Highway 88 provide access to the Mokelumne Wilderness (see Chapter 6 for background information), an area of stark granite expanses and lovely alpine lakes. Trails are delightfully uncrowded here, and Carson Pass is a great place to escape the Tahoe throngs for some quiet hiking. You won't need a permit for day hikes off Highway 88, but you may want to check at the information booth at the Carson Pass Summit for maps or current trail condition news. If you need an overnight permit or want to write for information in advance, contact the Toiyabe National Forest, Carson Ranger District, 1536 S Carson Street, Carson City, Nevada 89701.

## CAMPGROUNDS

**South Shore Campground** *(Hike 48, Devils Lake; Hike 49, Shriner Lake)*   Set above the shoreline of the Bear River Reservoir, the small South Shore Campground offers great access to a lot of recreation opportunities. There's swimming, boating, and fishing at the reservoir, and the campground isn't too far from the trailheads for Devils and Shriner lakes.

To reach South Shore Campground, turn off Highway 88 for Bear River Reservoir. Keep right at the first junction, and arrive at the campground 3.4 miles from Highway 88.

There are 22 campsites here (only nine are suitable for motorhomes). The campground has drinking water, picnic tables, fireplaces, and non-flush toilets. Open June to November. No reservations. Moderate fee.

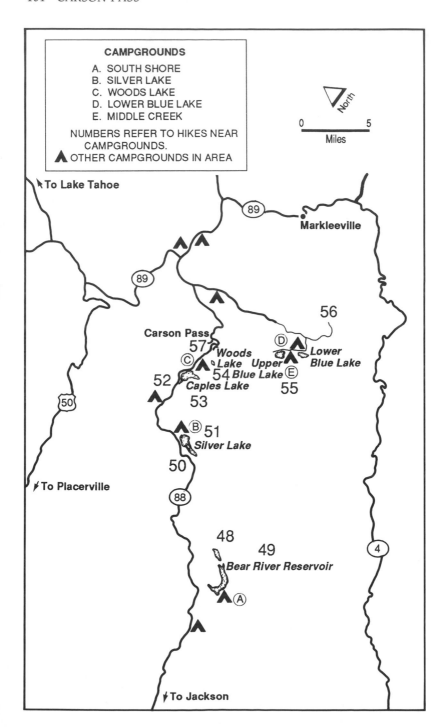

**Silver Lake Campground** *(Hike 50, Shealor Lake; Hike 51, Granite Lake and Hidden Lake)*   Vast and usually busy Silver Lake Campground is situated on the east shore of Silver Lake, with access to the water via a short footpath. A host of red firs shade the 100 spacious sites for tents and motorhomes, and campspots boast drinking water, fireplaces, picnic tables, and non-flush toilets.

Come early if you want a spot on the weekend. The campground is open June to November. No reservations. Moderate fee.

**Woods Lake Campground** *(Hike 52, Lake Margaret; Hike 53, Emigrant Lake; Hike 54, Round Top)*   The pleasant and popular Woods Lake Campground holds the trailhead for Hike 54, Round Top. To find the campground, drive 1.0 mile west of the Carson Pass Summit on Highway 88, and turn off for Woods Lake onto an unpaved

*A 10,390-foot-high picnic spot awaits on the summit of Round Top.*

road. Drive 0.4 mile and go left at a sign for Woods Lake. Continue 0.6 mile to the campground entrance.

If you're coming from the direction of Caples Lake, drive 2.2 miles east of the Caples Lake Resort turnoff on Highway 88, and go right for Woods Lake, 1.6 miles from the campground. Woods Lake Campground is a pleasant spot with 14 shaded sites for tents or motorhomes. Picnic tables, fireplaces, drinking water, and non-flush toilets are provided. Some campspots boast great views of Round Top, and all are near Woods Lake.

The campground is also very close to Carson Pass Summit, and no one driving Highway 88 should cruise through without pausing at the summit once. This isn't a roadside pullout—it's an educational experience. There's a Forest Service information booth here, manned by volunteers between Memorial Day and Labor Day. The summit also holds a replica of the famous Kit Carson Tree (the original is in Sutter's Fort in Sacramento) and an informational plaque about the well-traveled mountain man who gave his name to Carson Pass.

Woods Lake Campground is open July to October. No reservations. Moderate fee.

**Lower Blue Lake Campground** *(Hike 55, Granite Lake; Hike 56, Raymond Lake)*   Lower Blue Lake Campground is a Pacific Gas and Electric (PG&E) facility on the shore of Lower Blue Lake. Sixteen roomy tentsites have drinking water, picnic tables, fireplaces, and non-flush toilets. Fishermen will love it here, and would-be hikers will find trailheads close at hand.

To reach Lower Blue Lake Campground, turn off Highway 88 at the sign for Blue Lakes. Drive the paved road 7.0 miles, then continue 4.6 miles without pavement to a junction signed for Blue Lakes. Go right here and reach the campground 0.1 mile later. Open June through September. No reservations. Moderate fee.

**Middle Creek Campground** *(Hike 55, Granite Lake; Hike 56, Raymond Lake)*   Another PG&E campground, adjacent to the trailhead for Granite Lake, the tiny Middle Creek Campground is strung out along one bank of Middle Creek. Find the trail to Granite Lake by simply crossing the creek at the gauging station in the campground.

The five tentsites at Middle Creek Campground offer drinking water, picnic tables, fireplaces, and non-flush toilets. To find the campground, turn off Highway 88 at the sign for Blue Lakes. Drive the paved road 7.0 miles, then continue 4.6 miles without pavement to a junction signed for Blue Lakes. Go right here and pass Lower Blue Lake before arriving at Middle Creek Campground 13.2 miles off Highway 88.

The campground is open June through September. No reservations. Moderate fee.

# 48 DEVILS LAKE

Distance: 2.2 miles round trip
Difficulty: Easy
Starting point: 7,020 feet
High point: 7,300 feet
Total climb: 500 feet
Map: USGS Bear River Reservoir 7.5'

This easy hike to Devils Lake is far enough off the beaten track that you probably won't have to contend with high-season crowds at any time. The trail is mellow enough for families with small children, and the lake makes a pleasant destination for a picnic or a lazy afternoon.

To reach the trailhead for Devils Lake, turn off Highway 88 for Bear River Reservoir. Keep right at the first junction, pass the South Shore Campground, then stay left for Bear River Group Campground. Keep to the main, paved road 6.9 miles from Highway 88, then go left at a sign for the Devils Lake trailhead, turning onto a rough, unpaved road. Continue following signs for Devils Lake, and reach the trailhead after 2.3 miles of unpaved road.

Begin walking at a sign for the Devils Lake Trail, setting out on a level path beneath a thick canopy of red firs. Scattered white firs and lodgepole pines add to the forest blend, and lupine is a colorful downstairs neighbor to the trees.

Cross a creek at 0.2 mile, then enter a more open area of granite and pinemat manzanita. Climb gently to regain the trees. The ascent intensifies at 0.6 mile. Work through five short switchbacks, and

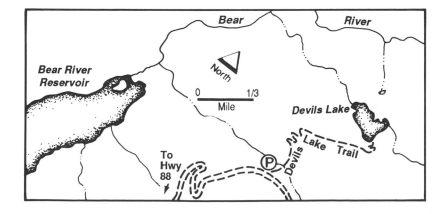

*A downhill finish marks the trek to Devils Lake.*

wind upward on a rocky trail lined with manzanita and canyon live oak.

Continue steadily uphill to cross an open hillside sprinkled with sturdy Jeffrey pines. A glance behind you will extend to the distant Bear River Reservoir. Reach the crest of the ridge at 0.9 mile, and take your first look at Devils Lake below. A steady, switchback-studded descent will take you to the shore of Devils Lake at 1.1 miles.

A handful of granite boulders in the center of this large lake,

combined with tree-lined shores and a quiet setting, make Devils
Lake a pleasant spot for picnicking or lounging away an afternoon.
There's nothing really spectacular about Devils Lake, but it's peaceful and little used. For a 2.2-mile investment in hiking, that's probably enough.

• • • • • • • • • • • • • • • • • • • • • • • • • • •

# 49 SHRINER LAKE

Distance: 4.2 miles round trip
Difficulty: Easy
Starting point: 6,470 feet
High point: 6,890 feet
Map: USGS Bear River Reservoir 7.5'

Like Devils Lake (Hike 48), Shriner Lake is a relatively undis-
covered and unvisited little pocket of Sierra scenery, easily reached
by a short, mellow trail. Children will enjoy this hike to attractive
Shriner Lake, and you can make the walk a learning experience by
pointing out the enormous variety of trees along the way.

To find the trailhead for Shriner Lake, turn off Highway 88
for Bear River Reservoir. Keep right at the first junction, pass the
South Shore Campground, then stay left for Bear River Group
Campground. Keep to the main, paved road 6.9 miles from Highway 88, then stay right with the paved route at the junction signed
for Shriner Trailhead.

Drive 3.2 miles past the junction, following signs for Cole
Creek, then turn left for the Shriner trailhead (10.1 miles off Highway 88). Drive the unpaved road 3.4 miles to an unsigned junction
and continue straight another 0.3 mile to the trailhead.

Begin at a sign for the Tanglefoot Trail, hiking gently uphill
on a dusty footpath. You'll have a lot of shade as you walk, thanks
to the presence of incense cedars, white firs, oaks, Jeffrey pines,
and even an occasional sugar pine. Bracken ferns are abundant on
the forest floor as well.

Reach an entry sign for the Mokelumne Wilderness at 0.4 mile,
and continue steadily up beneath the trees. Wind through a whispering stand of quaking aspens at 0.7 mile. The incline mellows
as you skirt beside a meadow glowing with California corn lily and
yampah.

Resume climbing to cross a low ridge at 0.9 mile. Hike beside
a small pond and a swampy meadow, then weave through an
outcropping of boulders at 1.1 miles. To the right is a good view

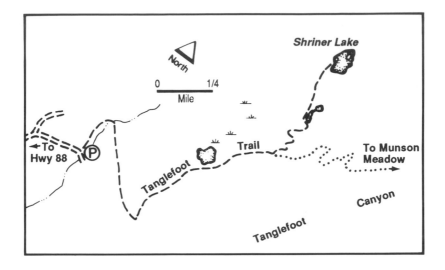

of Mokelumne Peak. Reach a junction signed for Munson Meadow and Shriner Lake at 1.4 miles, and go left for Shriner Lake.

Enjoy level walking through the trees, and pass another pocket-sized meadow before climbing again. Pass another small pond. A brief ascent leads into more level walking. Arrive at the shore of midsized Shriner Lake at 2.1 miles.

There's a sturdy, much-initialed picnic table on the lakeshore (a Boy Scout project, perhaps), and Mokelumne Peak rules the view out across the water. With a granite-ringed shoreline and several good swimming spots, Shriner Lake makes an excellent destination on a sunny afternoon.

## 50   SHEALOR LAKE

Distance: 2.8 miles round trip
Difficulty: Easy
Starting point: 7,410 feet
High point: 7,700 feet
Total climb: 840 feet
Map: USGS Tragedy Spring 7.5'

It's hard to say enough about the hike to Shealor Lake. How can such a short walk lead to such a tantalizing spot? But it does! Invest an afternoon at Shealor Lake—or take an entire day to make

*View from ridge above Shealor Lake*

this little jaunt. Whatever you give this lake in time and energy, it will amply reward you with striking scenery and rugged alpine beauty.

To reach the trailhead for Shealor Lake, drive Highway 88 1.2 miles west of the Kit Carson Lodge turnoff on the east shore of Silver Lake or 0.5 mile east of the Plasse Road turnoff when approaching Silver Lake from the west. Watch for a sign for Shealor Lakes. There's a parking area just off Highway 88.

Begin climbing through lodgepole pines and red firs, then start working upward across a granite-studded slope. This trail to Shealor Lake has two modes—up and down. The up lasts for the first 0.5 mile, then the down takes over.

The grade is moderate but unrelenting as you climb through a rocky landscape with intermittent trees and numerous hearty manzanita. Look for stunted lodgepole pines and tenacious Sierra junipers clinging to the granite slopes. Because the trail is difficult to follow through the rocks, you'll need to keep a sharp eye out for telltale ducks. Reach the crest of the ridge at 0.5 mile.

What a view! From here, look northward into the Desolation Wilderness, with lofty Pyramid Peak the major landmark. Vistas extend to the west and east as well, and there is a bird's-eye view down to Silver Lake.

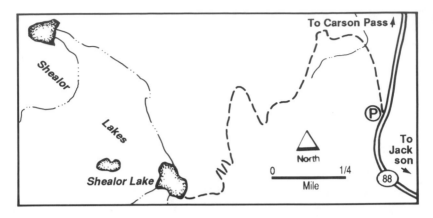

Shift gears as you begin the second part of this hike (the down), and savor the vista of Shealor Lake below. Descend a steep granite slope sprinkled with shaggy old Sierra junipers and hefty Jeffrey pines. The rough, zigzagging descent boasts 12 long switchbacks, with a lot of slow and tedious winding through the rocks.

Treat yourself to views of ruggedly handsome Shealor Lake and its granite-floored canyon as you pick your way downhill. Reach the lakeshore after 1.4 miles. This is an exceptionally scenic Sierra lake, a deep, watery hollow in a bed of solid granite.

One end of the lake boasts a line of vertical granite cliffs that rise more than 50 feet above the water. The other end offers campspots and picnicking. There are a host of excellent swimming spots as well. The lake temperature is agreeable, and staggered granite benches drop down into deep, clear water. Shealor Lake is simply wonderful.

• • • • • • • • • • • • • • • • • • • • • • •

# 51 GRANITE AND HIDDEN LAKES

Distance: 6.4 miles round trip
Difficulty: Moderate
Starting point: 7,300 feet
High point: 7,720 feet
Map: USGS Caples Lake 7.5'

The very short, but very scenic hike to Granite Lake (2.0 miles round trip) can be extended to a 6.4-mile jaunt by including Hidden Lake in the itinerary. Unfortunately (or fortunately, if you're looking for an easy hike) Hidden Lake is really nothing special, and the trail beyond Granite Lake is often dusty and busy with horses. The whole loop is included here, but it is best to just consider the trip to Granite Lake if you're short on time or energy.

To reach the trailhead for Granite Lake, turn off Highway 88 at the north end of Silver Lake at the sign for the Kit Carson Lodge. Drive the paved road past the lodge and follow signs for "Campfire Girls," going left at the first signed junction, then right at the second. Reach the trailhead after 1.4 miles.

Begin at a sign for the Minkalo Trail/Granite Lake, and start climbing on an exceedingly rocky trail lined with pinemat manzanita and lodgepole and Jeffrey pines. On a summer afternoon, you might witness a string of horses literally skate up this trail. The massive shelves of granite are definitely not "user friendly" to visitors with hooves.

You'll feel like you're hiking through an unseen giant's abandoned game of marbles as you traverse a landscape studded with countless scattered boulders, perched atop flat shelves of granite. These glacial erratics were left behind by traveling glaciers thousands of years ago, and they give evidence of the glacier-dominated geologic history of the Sierra Nevada Mountains.

Pick up views of Silver Lake as you ascend. The path is difficult to follow through the granite, so watch for ducks to keep track of the route. Gain level walking at the 0.3-mile point, then cross a seasonal creek on a wooden bridge soon after. A junction with a trail signed for Plasse is just beyond. Continue straight for Granite Lake.

Resume climbing through a granitic landscape sprinkled with tenacious manzanita and canyon live oak. Intermittent level stretches lead through Jeffrey and lodgepole pines and mountain hemlocks. Arrive at the shore of Granite Lake at 1.0 mile.

This is a gorgeous midsized lake, with deep water that's very inviting on a hot Sierra afternoon. If you're feeling unambitious, take the rest of the afternoon off and enjoy a leisurely picnic and

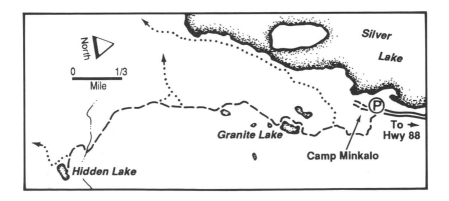

perhaps a swim. You won't find a nicer spot on this hike than Granite Lake.

To press on for Hidden Lake, stay with the main trail along the shore of Granite Lake and arrive at a sign for Hidden Lake. Continue curving around the shore, then leave Granite Lake at 1.2 miles. Traverse a level, tree-shaded landscape, interspersed with occasional outbursts of barren granite.

Cross a seasonal stream at 1.8 miles, then hike through a meadow that holds a wealth of alpine gentian and California corn lily. Reach a junction at 2.0 miles and keep to the left for Hidden Lake. Climb gently for a time, then gain more level walking through trees. The trail is very dusty here, tormented with the passage of an overabundance of horses. Your ascent to Hidden Lake begins as you cross a small stream at 3.0 miles. Reach the shore of the small lake at 3.2 miles. It's shallow and not too scenic, so "hoof it" back to Granite Lake if you're looking for a spot to spend a lazy hour.

• • • • • • • • • • • • • • • • • • • • • • • •

# 52  LAKE MARGARET

Distance: 4.8 miles round trip
Difficulty: Easy
Starting point: 7,700 feet
High point: 7,700 feet
Total climb: 590 feet
Map: USGS Caples Lake 7.5'

The short jaunt to the shore of Lake Margaret is an easy family hike. It's a pleasant walk, made even nicer with the company of pretty Caples Creek, and little Lake Margaret is a wonderful spot to spread a picnic or plunk in a fishing line.

To find the trailhead for Lake Margaret, turn off Highway 88 1.1 miles west of the Caples Lake Resort turnoff. A sign beside Highway 88 calls out Lake Margaret, and there is ample trailhead parking just off the main road.

Begin at a trail sign for Lake Margaret and descend through lodgepole pines and mountain hemlocks as you set out. An undulating trail leads on through a granite landscape, then into trees again. You'll cross a small stream at 0.5 mile, then pass a short turnoff trail to the right that leads to the banks of Caples Creek.

This pristine little waterway is worth a visit. Clear and cold with a pebbly bottom, it's deep enough to tempt would-be swimmers and pretty enough to make one want to linger; however, there's time for that on the way back. Continue with the main trail to reach a bridge across Caples Creek at 0.7 mile.

Cross the creek, then look for blazes on the trees as you hike through a lodgepole pine forest before climbing into a rocky landscape layered with pinemat manzanita and canyon live oak. You'll arrive at a granite-overhung pond at 1.1 miles. Continue on the trail, watching for ducks when the way is indistinct through the rocks.

Pass a second, larger pond at 1.4 miles, then enjoy level walking through a forest where tall red firs cast their shade toward a California corn lily carpeted earth. You'll enter a wonderful expanse of lupine at 1.9 miles. Then a lush jungle of cow parsnip and Sierra alders beckons as you walk beside a seasonal stream. (Note: at the height of mosquito season, this stretch can be miserable.)

Cross the stream on a large tree trunk at 2.2 miles, then wind on through a grove of quaking aspens to a final brief ascent up a granite-covered hillside. Keep an eye out for patches of fragrant wild spearmint as you climb. Arrive on the shore of Margaret Lake at 2.4 miles.

With granite-scattered shores, a deep center, and a handful of pretty rock islands in the middle, Margaret Lake is a delightful

*Lake Margaret is a wonderful family destination.*

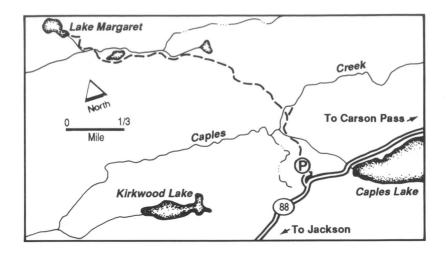

destination. There's fishing and camping to tempt the long-term visitor, and there are a lot of picnic spots for those with only an afternoon to spare.

• • • • • • • • • • • • • • • • • • • • • • • • •

# 53    EMIGRANT LAKE

Distance: 8.8 miles round trip
Difficulty: Moderate
Starting point: 7,800 feet
High point: 8,600 feet
Map: USGS Caples Lake 7.5′

This hike to Emigrant Lake has several things going for it. It has a trailhead just off Highway 88, so it's very easy to reach. Nearly the entire trail is through trees, so it's an excellent hot-day hike. The trail is steeped in Sierra Nevada history, as it traverses some of the routes taken by the early emigrant parties that struggled through the Carson Pass area.

To reach the trailhead for Emigrant Lake, drive 0.9 mile west of the Caples Lake Resort turnoff on Highway 88. Turn into the large, paved parking area signed for Caples Lake. There are bathrooms at the trailhead.

Begin walking at a sign for the Emigrant Lake Trail. You'll be entering the Mokelumne Wilderness as you set out along the shore

*A pleasant trail leads to the shore of Emigrant Lake.*

of the vast Caples Lake, an immensely popular spot with vacationing fishermen. Walk in the shade of lodgepole pines and mountain hemlocks as you trace the level trail just above the lake.

A bit of traffic noise will drift across the water from Highway 88, but it can't spoil the beauty of the forest or the wildflowers along the trail. Reach a junction with the Old Emigrant Road at the 1.3-mile point. This historic route takes off up the hillside, but you'll keep to the level main trail along the lake.

Draw even with the end of Caples Lake at 2.0 miles, and continue level walking through a forest brightened by California corn lily, yampah, pearly everlasting, and a lot of lupine. The climb toward Emigrant Lake commences at 2.6 miles as you ascend beside a seasonal stream. Climb steadily for about half a mile, then a brief level section will lead into still more climbing.

Wind upward through a boulder-sprinkled landscape, enjoying the shade of lodgepole pines, western white pines, and mountain hemlocks. Cross Emigrant Lake's outlet stream at 3.7 miles. The pink monkeyflower, ranger buttons, crimson columbine, and swamp onion that make its banks a parade of colors may tempt

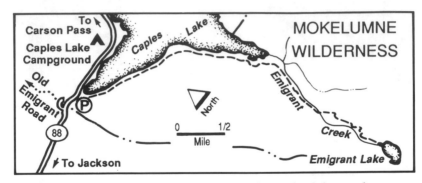

you to linger here, but now you're nearly to the lake, so keep on climbing.

Continue up the hillside, keeping with the main trail (foot trails veer off to campspots). The ascent switchbacks, with views down to Caples Lake snatched from between the trees. The terrain levels off as you approach Emigrant Lake along the edge of a delightful meadow. Arrive on the lakeshore at 4.4 miles.

Backed by a ring of granite cliffs, Emigrant Lake is deep and inviting, rich in fishing spots, picnic sites, and scenery. You'll see 9,565-foot Covered Wagon Peak on the ridge above the lake. Covered Wagon Peak was the highest point reached by covered wagons on the emigrants' journey west.

Settle back and imagine days long past, then journey back to the present for a picnic or a swim before hitting the trail for your return trip.

• • • • • • • • • • • • • • • • • • • • • • •

# 54 ROUND TOP

Distance: 6.4 miles (loop)
Difficulty: Strenuous
Starting point: 8,220 feet
High point: 10,390 feet
Maps: USGS Caples Lake 7.5' and USGS Carson Pass 7.5'

You'll have to look long and hard to find a day hike more full of lakes and vistas than this loop walk, which encompasses a trip to the summit of Round Top. It's only 6.4 miles, but you'll certainly feel the strain, as the scramble to the summit of the peak is steep and challenging. Be sure to bring a jacket and plenty of water for the top.

*Weary hikers rest and enjoy the summit of Round Top.*

To reach the trailhead, follow directions to the Woods Lake Campground provided in this chapter's campground section. Non-camping visitors should park in the campground's day-use/picnic area. A sign at the nearby trailhead identifies the Winnemucca Lake Trail.

Start off by crossing the creek on a sturdy bridge and following the trail sign into a sparse forest of western white pines, lodgepole pines, and mountain hemlocks. Climb gently with views of Round Top through the trees. Look for hardy pinemat manzanita in the rocky sections, and enjoy lupine, California corn lily, yampah, and nude buckwheat along the way.

Keep an eye out for the remnants of a rock-crushing device used in mining operations at the 0.8-mile point. After about a mile, begin to work your way across an open slope with a lot of sage and Indian paintbrush, then reach a sign marking your entry into the Mokelumne Wilderness at 1.1 miles. Climb beside a small stream as you savor wonderful views of Round Top straight ahead.

Reach the shore of Winnemucca Lake at 1.6 miles. This large lake is deep and very clear, with an attractive backdrop of tumbling granite. Take the path for Round Top Lake to continue. Cross a small stream and climb along a rocky hillside, then cross another stream lined with brilliant yellow alpine monkeyflower and Sierra arnica.

Continue steadily up with nice views back to Winnemucca Lake. The terrain levels out just before Round Top Lake at 2.5 miles. Round Top Lake is smaller than Winnemucca and it's not as scenic, but this is where the side trail takes off toward the summit of Round Top.

Without this little summit jaunt, the loop we describe here is an easy 4.6 miles and an excellent family hike. With the climb to Round Top, the hike's difficulty increases dramatically—but so does its appeal.

To make the trip to Round Top's top, veer left just before Round Top Lake, and follow an unsigned use trail that heads off toward the peak. Stay with the trail on the left side of the creek gully, climbing steeply with views behind all the way down to Caples Lake. The terrain is rocky and the footing will only get worse from here (but the views will only get more breathtaking).

The main trail is joined by several other use trails as it climbs, and the incline gains intensity with each step. Look for scattered stunted whitebark pines, a lot of Brewer's lupine, and the ever-present sage. A saddle marks 3.1 miles. The climb from here is agonizingly steep, and the footing is bad at best.

Take it slow and pause to suck in lungfuls of air as you savor the expanding view. You'll reach the lower of Round Top's double summits at 3.4 miles. The trek to the higher knob involves some

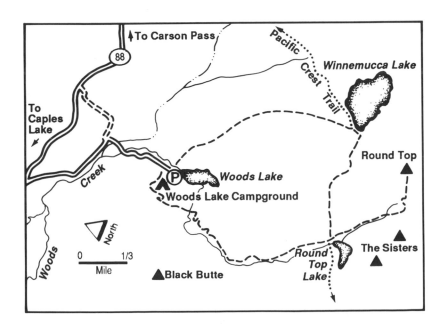

tricky climbing, so don't try it unless you're sure-footed and un-afraid of heights. There is a climbers' register in a metal cylinder atop the knob.

From either spot, the view is awesome, extending to Lake Tahoe in the north and The Dardanelles to the south. Look for Blue Lakes and Lost Lake on one side; Caples Lake, Woods Lake, Round Top Lake, Winnemucca Lake, and Frog Lake on the other. If you have a topo map along, you should be able to identify several surrounding peaks.

When you're finally able to tear your eyes from the view, scramble down the hill to Round Top Lake to resume your loop, then take the trail to the north for Woods Lake and descend steadily across an open hillside. The terrain levels out as you traverse a lush meadow sewn through with ranger buttons.

Come in beside a creek at 4.8 miles and leave the Mokelumne Wilderness soon after. Descend beside the water, walking in the shade of mountain hemlocks and western white pines. Notice evidence of a small mining operation at 5.4 miles—an old shack, a rusted car, and a no trespassing sign. This is an active claim, so the sign should be heeded.

Walk steadily downhill and cross the creek at 5.6 miles. You'll have glimpses down to Woods Lake as you continue. Walk a rough four-wheel-drive road for the last leg of your loop, and arrive at the paved campground road at 6.2 miles. Go right here, and follow signs back to the day-use parking area to close your circle at 6.4 miles.

## 55  GRANITE LAKE

Distance: 4.0 miles round trip
Difficulty: Easy
Starting point: 8,120 feet
High point: 8,700 feet
Maps: USGS Pacific Valley 7.5' and
  USGS Carson Pass 7.5'

*Sierra junipers*

Considering the small investment in time and energy required to hike to Granite Lake, this walk pays some of the highest dividends of any trek off Carson Pass. Granite Lake is a delightful alpine gem, and the view from the ridge near the water is one you

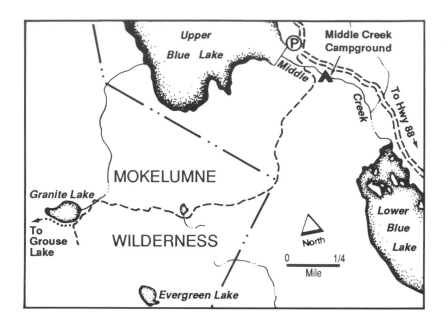

won't soon forget. With its mellow inclines and wonderful destination, this walk makes a perfect family outing.

To reach the trailhead for Granite Lake, turn off Highway 88 at the sign for Blue Lakes. Drive the paved road 7.0 miles, then continue 4.6 miles without pavement to a junction signed for Blue Lakes. Turn right here and pass Lower Blue Lake and Middle Creek Campground. The trailhead for the Grouse Lake Trail is 0.2 mile beyond Middle Creek Campground. (Total distance from Highway 88 is 13.4 miles.)

Begin on the shaded Grouse Lake Trail, walking beneath lodgepole pines and mountain hemlocks. Cross Middle Creek on a log bridge at 0.1 mile, and continue downstream, staying with the main trail as a secondary route joins in from the campground just across the water.

Angle away from Middle Creek on a trail lined with yampah and California corn lily, and begin a gentle climb toward Granite Lake. You'll enjoy a host of wildflowers if you're hiking early in the season. Follow a forested ridgeline gently upward to arrive at a sign for the Grouse Lake Trail at 0.9 mile.

Continue straight for Grouse Lake and enter the Mokelumne Wilderness soon after. An easy ascent leads upward through red firs, western white pines, lodgepole pines, and mountain hemlocks, then you'll begin a winding trek through a dry granitic landscape. The vista to the right takes in Upper Blue Lake.

Reach a small pond at 1.3 miles and climb more steeply for a while. The incline mellows once again as you traverse an open granite landscape dotted with mountain hemlocks and low-lying lupine. Note the pinkish hue of the surrounding rocks.

Climb beside a small seasonal stream with banks overflowing with wildflowers, and arrive on the shore of Granite Lake at 2.0 miles. Deep and lovely Granite Lake is aptly named, surrounded by granite slopes and perched atop a rocky ridgetop. Its cool water offers invigorating swimming possibilities, and its grassy shores boast yampah, mountain pennyroyal, California corn lily, and abundant Brewer's lupine.

After you've enjoyed the lake awhile, find a great viewspot by continuing with the trail along the shoreline. Cut left away from the lake just beyond a granite outcropping. Walk up the small draw and angle right at the crest of the ridge to climb to the top of a small rock outcropping (0.1 mile from the lakeshore).

The view from here encompasses Meadow Lake and the North Fork of the Mokelumne River to the right; Evergreen Lake, Silver and Highland peaks, and Raymond and Reynolds peaks to the left. It's definitely worth the short excursion.

• • • • • • • • • • • • • • • • • • • • • • • • • • •

# 56 RAYMOND LAKE

Distance: 11.2 miles round trip
Difficulty: Strenuous
Starting point: 7,870 feet
High point: 9,000 feet
Total climb: 3,120 feet
Maps: USGS Pacific Valley 7.5' and USGS Ebbetts Pass 7.5'

This challenging hike to Raymond Lake is not for early season visitors, not for children, and definitely not for the timid. The hike is long, and this section of the Pacific Crest Trail (PCT) traverses steeply sloped hillsides that are extremely treacherous when snow is present. Wait until the snow is gone, plan to take an entire day to do the hike, and then look forward to some enchanting and extremely scenic walking.

To reach the trailhead for Raymond Lake, turn off Highway 88 at the sign for Blue Lakes. Drive the paved road 7.0 miles, and continue 3.6 miles without pavement to a turnoff signed for Tamarack Lake/Wet Meadows. Go left on the rough, unpaved Road 097, and drive 3.1 miles to a junction signed for Lower Sunset Lake. Go left here and drive 0.1 mile to an unsigned trailhead (just before Lower Sunset Lake) marked by small rock cairns on either side of the road.

Set out on the trail that takes off from the right-hand (south) side of the road, hiking a dusty route through sage, mule ears, and mountain pennyroyal, beneath a scattering of lodgepole pines. Climb gently and cross a four-wheel-drive road. Views below are of Lower Sunset Lake.

As the undulating trail continues, you'll see several seasonal streams amid a varied forest of mountain hemlocks, Sierra junipers, and red firs. Merge with a use trail from a nearby meadow at 1.0 mile. Continue to the left, passing a small pond as you go. If you're hiking in August, you'll notice cows (or their footprints—or worse) in the meadowy areas along the trail.

Cross an intersecting four-wheel-drive road at 1.5 miles. Pacific Crest Trail markers identify the trail. Begin descending beside a seasonal stream, and keep to the right with the PCT when the trail branches. Cross a creek at the bottom of the gully at 1.9 miles. This monkeyflower-lined waterway could be a real roarer in early season.

Angle to the left away from the water, looking for blazes on the trees to help you find the trail. Wind on through a deep red fir forest, and reach a junction with the Pleasant Valley Trail at 2.3 miles. Stay with the PCT as you go right and begin to climb at a steady pace. You'll get views of Pleasant Valley and The Nipple (you'll know it when you see it!) as you climb.

Make three long switchbacks to reach the crest of the hill at 2.9 miles. From here the trail continues across the steep hillsides beyond. Work across an open, rocky hillside with a lot of sage and mountain pennyroyal. The view extends all the way to Markleeville.

Cross a creek that's a housing development for deep blue tower larkspur, and continue along the hillside to reach Raymond Lake's

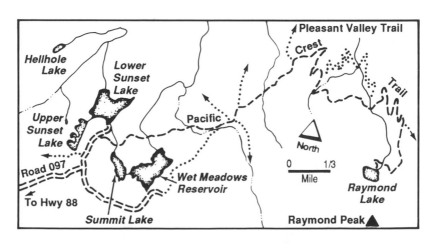

*A hiker makes the 3,120-foot ascent to Raymond Lake.*

outlet creek at 3.8 miles. Willows and ranger buttons are abundant here. Begin the ascent of the canyon wall, climbing in long switch-backs with a steadily expanding view.

You'll leave a thick stand of red firs, western white pines, and mountain hemlocks and emerge onto an open hillside that's a gorgeous mix of mule ears, lupine, and sage. Continue steadily up to reach the turnoff trail for Raymond Lake at 4.8 miles. Go right and abandon the PCT, enjoying fine views of 10,014-foot Raymond Peak.

Cross a seasonal stream, then begin a final uphill push that leads to the shore of rugged Raymond Lake at 5.6 miles. One look at this 9,000-foot-high alpine gem, and you'll know immediately that it was worth the climb.

Raymond Lake sits cradled within a semicircle of nearly vertical slopes, nestled into the bosom of jagged Raymond Peak. It has a rocky shore dotted with mountain hemlocks and whitebark pines, and its water is deep enough for swimming, although it may be cold enough to demand a wet suit on most days. Unpack your lunch and linger long enough to let your legs recuperate.

# 57 MEISS LAKE

Distance: 8.0 miles round trip
Difficulty: Moderate
Starting point: 8,560 feet
High point: 8,790 feet
Total climb: 880 feet
Maps: USGS Caples Lake 7.5' and USGS Carson Pass 7.5'

Only the length of this trek to Meiss Lake keeps it from ranking as an easy hike. It's mostly mellow meadow walking. That's unusual, considering this is a section of the notoriously rugged Pacific Crest Trail. Try to visit Meiss Lake as early in the season as the snows allow, as heavy grazing decimates the meadow wildflowers every year. And come on a weekday if possible. Weekends are busy, busy, busy here.

To reach the trailhead for Meiss Lake, drive 0.2 mile west of the Carson Pass Summit on Highway 88. There's a large parking area on the north side of the road. It's unsigned as of this writing, as is the trailhead itself. The trail takes off from the parking area.

Begin with a gentle climb as you traverse an open hillside sprinkled with Sierra junipers and lodgepole pines. Watch for mule ears, sage, and nude buckwheat in the dry soil along the trail. As the trail levels off along the hill, fine views of Elephants Back and Round Top (Hike 54) emerge.

Skirt along a hillside rich in mountain pennyroyal, scarlet gilia, and Indian paintbrush, and pick up views of Caples Lake and Covered Wagon Peak as you continue. Cross a seasonal stream at 1.0 mile, then cross a second stream soon after. The uphill grade increases as the trail angles toward the ridgetop through a herd of fuzzy-leaved mule ears.

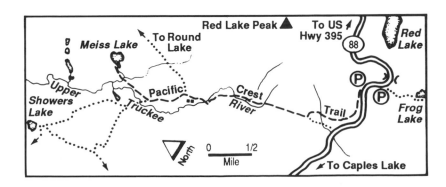

Merge with a steeper, shorter trail joining from an alternate trailhead at 1.2 miles, and continue up to cross a barbed-wire fence at 1.4 miles. The grade mellows a bit as you cross the broad ridgetop. Wild iris is abundant early in the season, and the views are marvelous all year.

Start downhill at 1.6 miles. You should be able to spot Lake Tahoe in the distance on a clear day, and you'll see numerous peaks jabbing the skyline to the north. Descend gradually and cross a small stream at 2.1 miles. Look for alpine monkeyflower and lupine on its banks.

Continue down into a vast meadow. By mid-August of each year, it's sadly scarred from heavy cattle grazing, and you'll have to search long and hard for remnants of the once abundant wildflowers if you come late in the season.

Cross a barbed-wire fence at 2.5 miles, then pass a cabin and a barn (to the left of the trail) and another fence at 2.8 miles. There is a junction with the trail for Round Lake soon after. Continue straight for Showers Lake, and enjoy the shade of scattered lodgepole pines as you hike on.

You'll spot the mirrorlike surface of Meiss Lake off to the right across the meadow as you walk. Several unmarked footpaths/cowpaths head off toward Meiss Lake from here on out. Wait for the turnoff trail that veers right just before the main trail crosses the Upper Truckee River at the 3.4-mile point (it's just a lazy creek here). Take the turnoff trail, and trace a meandering path across the meadow toward Meiss Lake.

To cross Meiss Lake's outlet stream as you near the lakeshore, abandon the trail and angle right. There's a shaky log spanning the water here. Continue on toward the lake and reach the grassy shore at 4.0 miles.

Midsized Meiss Lake is surprisingly shallow, with its deepest point about 9 feet. It does offer a pretty shoreline and a fine view out across the meadow. Recently replanted with cutthroat trout, the lake is a pleasant destination spot for fishing, wildflower watching, and peaceful picnicking.

# CHAPTER EIGHT
· · · · · · · · ·
# Echo Pass (Highway 50)

The Echo Pass area suffers from its easy accessibility and its proximity to Lake Tahoe. It's crowded on summer weekends, and even weekdays bring more people to the trailheads than the areas south to Yosemite National Park entertain. Despite its popularity, Echo Pass is worth exploring. There are some wonderful hikes to discover here. Just be prepared to share them.

Because this is a high-use area, all hikes in this chapter (except Hike 64, Dardanelles Lake) require day-hiking permits. At present,

*Echo Lake on the trail to Ralston Lake*

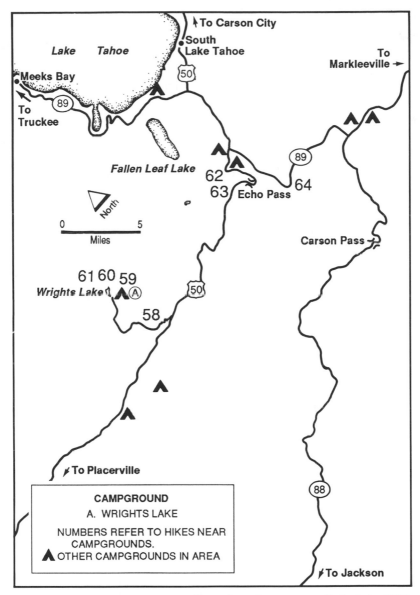

there is no quota system in effect, but there was talk in late 1989 of changing that situation. Many of the trailheads offer self-issue permits on-site. However, it's a good idea to obtain your permit in advance (and check on changes in regulations) at a Forest Service office.

You can get day-hiking permits at the Lake Tahoe Visitors Information Center. It's just off Highway 89, 3.1 miles west of its

*Lyons Lake is an enchanting corner of the Sierra Nevada.*

junction with Highway 50. Permits are also available at the Lake Tahoe Basin Management Unit, PO Box 731002, 870 Emerald Bay Road, South Lake Tahoe, California 95731. Or, if you're approaching from the west on Highway 50, get your permit at either the Eldorado National Forest Office, 100 Forni Road, Placerville, California 95667, or the Pacific Ranger Station, Pollock Pines, California 95726.

Echo Pass provides access to the 63,000-acre Desolation Wilderness, an enchanting corner of the Sierra, bordered on the east by Lake Tahoe and on the south by Highway 50. The Desolation Wilderness is remarkable for its multitude of lakes (more than 120 of them) and for its accessibility, although some might view this as a curse rather than a blessing. Whatever, it's a wilderness that's easy to get to and easy to explore, and that makes for wonderful hiking.

## CAMPGROUNDS

**Wrights Lake Campground** (*Hike 58, Lyons Lake; Hike 59, Smith Lake; Hike 60, Twin Lakes; Hike 61, Gertrude Lake*)  Campgrounds are scarce on Echo Pass, but this large facility beside Wrights Lake provides excellent access to four of the hikes in this section.

Wrights Lake Campground offers drinking water, fireplaces, picnic tables, and non-flush toilets. Sites overlook Wrights Lake, where recreation opportunities abound (fishing, boating, swimming, hiking, etc.).

Unfortunately, this is an exceedingly busy campground, despite its more than 70 spots for tents or motorhomes. You'll almost always need reservations to claim a weekend site. Call the Forest Service's (800) 280-CAMP number well in advance of your intended visit.

To find Wrights Lake Campground, turn off Highway 50 for Wrights Lake 13 miles west of Echo Pass Summit or 36 miles east of the Highway 49 junction in Placerville, and drive 8.1 miles on a paved road to reach the campground entrance. Open June through October. Reservations accepted. Moderate fee.

• • • • • • • • • • • • • • • • • • • • • • • • • • • •

# 58   LYONS LAKE

Distance: 9.8 miles round trip
Difficulty: Strenuous
Starting point: 6,720 feet
High point: 8,390 feet
Map: USGS Pyramid Peak 7.5'

Except for a truly gruesome final pitch, this hike to Lyons Lake is a fairly mellow trek beside lovely Lyons Creek. Even with the hill, the trip's final destination is so spectacular that any complainers in your party will quickly be consoled. There were plans afoot for extensive trail work on this route in 1989, so don't be surprised if if you find a few variations from our description.

To reach the trailhead for Lyons Lake, turn off Highway 50 for Wrights Lake and drive 4.1 miles on a paved road, then turn right at a sign for the Lyons Creek Trailhead. Continue 0.5 mile on unpaved road to find your starting point.

Set off on a gently climbing trail beneath lodgepole pines and mountain hemlocks, and look for lupine and mountain pennyroyal on the forest floor. You'll be ascending beside Lyons Creek for this entire hike. It's a pretty little waterway, cut through granite slabs and tumbled rocks.

If you're walking in late summer, you may spot a lot of cattle on this trek. They're a good reminder of why it's generally unsafe to drink from even the most sparkling Sierra creek. The presence of *Giardia* is too great of a risk.

Cross several seasonal streams as you continue, with views ahead of striking Pyramid Peak. Arrive at a junction with the trail to Bloodsucker and Wrights Lake (left). Continue straight for Lyons

Lake, climbing gently as you leave the junction.

Reach an entry sign for the Desolation Wilderness at 2.9 miles, then work your way into a more rocky area boasting western white pines, canyon live oak, and pinemat manzanita. The climb beside Lyons Creek continues, and you'll reenter a lodgepole pine forest not long after.

Start across another rocky section at 3.3 miles. The grade increases for a time, then mellows at the 3.7-mile point. Traverse a rugged slope with excellent views ahead to Pyramid Peak, and cross Lyons Creek at 4.2 miles. Continue uphill to a junction at 4.3 miles.

The trail to Lake Sylvia goes on for 0.4 mile from here. This is a pleasant destination if you wish to avoid the punishing pitch to Lyons Lake. If you're willing to sweat for some super scenery, however, go left at the junction and proceed to Lyons Lake.

At first, the climb is moderate, but the ascent gains intensity as you scramble upward through the rocks. Struggle up beside Lyons Lake's plummeting outlet stream, scanning for ducks and blazes to help you find the way. The climb is gruesome, but it's mercifully brief.

Reach a lower pool at 4.8 miles, and continue past a handsome old rock dam to gain the shore of Lyons Lake at 4.9 miles. This is a gorgeous spot! Lyons Lake commands a spectacular site, tucked within an amphitheater of granite. Sturdy mountain hemlocks crowd the shoreline, and there are some excellent spots for swimming, if you don't mind chilly water.

If you're fortunate, you'll have this lonely little masterpiece all to yourself. Savor a picnic with the scenery, then scramble down the hill toward home.

• • • • • • • • • • • • • • • • • • • • • • • •

# 59   SMITH LAKE

Distance: 6.2 miles round trip
Difficulty: Strenuous
Starting point: 6,950 feet
High point: 8,700 feet
Map: USGS Pyramid Peak 7.5′

If you're a lake lover, you won't find many hikes more loaded with lakes than this one. Not only will you visit Grouse Lake, you'll climb to Hemlock Lake and Smith Lake as well. And each of these lakes is more than worth the sometimes arduous ascent.

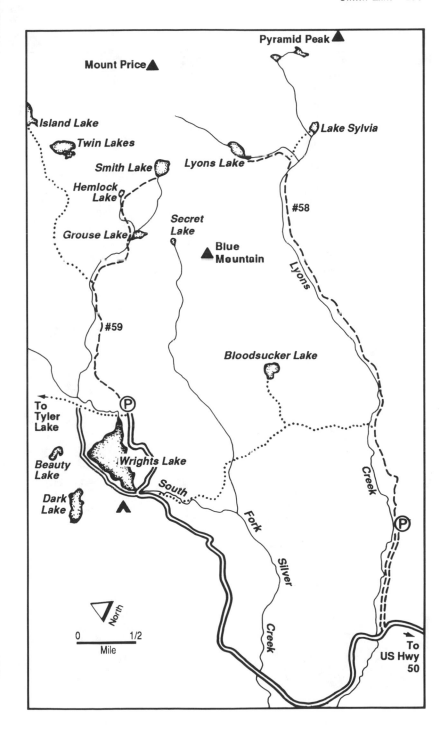

*Lofty Smith Lake is a striking spot to linger and enjoy.*

This is a very popular area, and a day-use hiking permit is required of all visitors. Self-issue permits are currently available at the ranger station beside Wrights Lake Campground.

To find the trailhead for Smith Lake, turn off Highway 50 for Wrights Lake and drive 8.1 miles on a paved road to reach a junction at Wrights Lake Campground. Pause here to claim your hiking permit, then turn right at the sign for the Twin and Grouse Lake Trail. Proceed another 1.0 mile to reach the day-use parking area.

Begin at the trailhead sign for the Twin and Grouse Lake Trail, and start your hike by crossing a barbed-wire fence, then cruise on beside a lush, wildflower-filled meadow. Cross a pair of seasonal streams, and climb to an unmarked trail junction at 0.5 mile. The spur trail leading to the left hooks up with the trail to Tyler Lake (Hike 61).

Continue to the right, ascending a granite-studded slope, then reentering trees for a time. The grade intensifies as you negotiate another rocky section, flecked with canyon live oak and pinemat manzanita. You'll gain views behind of Wrights Lake as you climb.

Cross a stream at 1.1 miles and climb to an entry sign for the Desolation Wilderness soon after. An unmarked trail takes off to the left from here, but keep right to continue on toward Grouse Lake, enjoying mellower hiking for a time. Reach a junction with the trail signed for Twin/Island Lake at 1.3 miles (Hike 60).

Go right on the Grouse/Hemlock Lake Trail, and climb steadily across an open granite slope, tracing a path outlined with rocks. As you gaze out across the broad granite canyon on the left, you'll have no trouble seeing how the Desolation Wilderness got its name. Continue up at an unrelenting pace. Mountain hemlocks and western white pines provide welcome snatches of shade.

You'll cross Grouse Lake's outlet stream at 2.0 miles, then climb steeply to reach Grouse Lake 0.2 mile later. This little grass-edged gem is particularly inviting after a stiff climb, and you'll probably be tempted to linger here; however, two more lakes await your visit.

Continue to the left around the shore, and angle away from the lake just before you cross an inlet stream. Slosh through a marshy area with cheery islands of California corn lily and alpine gentian, then resume climbing at a challenging grade. If you need to stop to catch your breath, look back for a fine view of Wrights Lake. The incline eases at 2.5 miles, and a rocky trail leads on to Hemlock Lake at 2.7 miles.

This petite pocket of blue is sewn into a glowing granite slope, bordered by sturdy mountain hemlocks and lovely mountain heather. Hemlock Lake may be shallow as far as water goes, but it's deep in scenic beauty. Wander along the shoreline to the right, then resume climbing on a heather-bordered trail.

The grade is gentle at first, but it soon picks up momentum

as you scramble up a rocky hillside. The vast Union Valley Reservoir comes into view as you gain elevation. Arrive at your third and final lake at 3.1 miles.

Enchanting Smith Lake seems like it's set right on top of the world, and chances are good you won't be able to resist its clear, cold water after the arduous climb you've just completed. Smith Lake's rugged granite shoreline crashes right into the sparkling water, and the setting here is lonely, stark, and strangely peaceful.

• • • • • • • • • • • • • • • • • • • • • • • • •

# 60 TWIN LAKES

Distance: 6.8 miles round trip
Difficulty: Moderate
Starting point: 6,950 feet
High point: 8,150 feet
Map: USGS Pyramid Peak 7.5'

Of the three hikes included for the Wrights Lake area, the trek to Twin Lakes is probably the busiest. If you're simply seeking solitude, Twin Lakes is not the spot to visit. But if you're looking for some spectacular Desolation Wilderness scenery without too much climbing, then put up with the crowds, put on your hiking boots, and go.

As with the hike to Smith Lake (Hike 59), a day-use permit is required for Twin Lakes. Refer to the first six paragraphs of Hike 59 to get you started on the Twin Lakes Trail. From the junction at the 1.3-mile point, go left to continue on toward Twin Lakes.

Climb gently through a granitic landscape dotted with feisty canyon live oak and pinemat manzanita. Cross a seasonal stream soon after, then begin a more noticeable ascent. Reach a ridgetop at 1.8 miles, and continue on a rock-lined trail. Enjoy level walking for 0.2 mile, then climb again through lots and lots of rocks.

Emerge into Twin Lakes' amazing granite basin at 2.3 miles. This wonderful corner of the Desolation Wilderness seems to be nothing but a giant saucer of glowing rock, given life by the single thread of water trickling downhill from lake to lake to lake. The stark beauty of the spot will lighten your footsteps as you continue on.

Follow the path of the water gently uphill, pacing across slabs of granite polished to a silky sheen by long-passed glaciers. The "trail" is traced out by double lines of rocks. Arrive on the shore

*The trail to Twin Lakes is outlined across solid stone.*

of Lower Twin Lake at 2.7 miles, and zig to the left to cross its outlet stream on a small rock dam.

Lower Twin Lake is large and inviting, but there are a host of tantalizing spots in this spectacular lake basin, all of them worth a stop. Continue with the path along the lakeshore, then angle away to climb gently toward Boomerang Lake. You'll reach this little L-shaped lake at 3.1 miles. It really does look like a boomerang!

Cruise onward on a trail edged with bright fireweed, lupine, spiraea, and ranger buttons. You'll marvel at the lushness of the granite-governed landscape as you hike on toward Island Lake. Pass a few small ponds along the way, and arrive at Island Lake at 3.4 miles.

Island Lake's long, shimmering surface is interrupted by a host of rocky islands. This is a great spot for a swim, if you don't mind chilly water. Or simply dabble your toes and let your eyes wade through the scenery, then spread out a picnic. You can also pass the afternoon exploring the enchanting Twin Lakes basin.

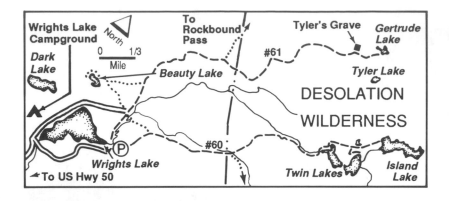

## 61   GERTRUDE LAKE

Distance: 8.2 miles round trip
Difficulty: Moderate
Starting point: 6,950 feet
High point: 8,000 feet
Maps: USGS Pyramid Peak 7.5' and
      USGS Rockbound Valley 7.5'

*Trail sign in the Wrights Lake area*

If you have several days to explore the trails around Wrights Lake, reserve an afternoon for the trek to Gertrude Lake. It's not as scenic as the hikes to Smith Lake or Twin Lakes (Hikes 59 and 60), but it's not as crowded either. If you're tired of the hordes, Gertrude Lake is the place to go.

As with the two earlier hikes mentioned, you'll need a day-use permit for this trek. Refer to the first three paragraphs of Hike 59 for information and directions to the trailhead. Currently, there is no identifying sign at the trailhead for this hike. From the day-use parking area, cross the creek on a wooden footbridge. Follow the trail to the right along the little waterway, enjoying the cheery company of Brewer's lupine and spiraea as you walk.

There is a fine view out across the lush meadow just across the creek. Look for the outline of 9,975-foot Mount Price above the clearing. Cross a barbed-wire fence at 0.3 mile, and continue with level walking on an old roadbed.

Reach a junction with a trail signed for Twin Lakes at 0.4 mile.

Continue straight for Maud Lake/Tyler Lake instead. (There's a trail to the left that leads to Beauty Lake as well.) Level walking continues as you pace beneath red firs and Jeffrey pines. Take the trail branching left off the road at the 0.6-mile point.

You'll merge with a trail from an alternate trailhead soon afterward. Continue straight as you hike through a lush forest carpeted with bracken ferns and lupine. Begin a gentle climb as you work into a granitic landscape colored with manzanita and canyon live oak, and endure a steady uphill course with fine views of surrounding peaks.

Descend briefly to a junction with the trail for Rockbound Pass at 1.8 miles. Keep to the right on the Tyler Lake Trail, and climb away from the junction to reach an entry sign for the Desolation Wilderness after 0.2 mile. Continue up through a rock-flecked landscape, moving away from mellow climbing into a steep ascent.

At 2.2 miles, gain the crest of the ridge and a nice vista of glowing granite slopes, backed by stern Mount Price. Enjoy a brief stretch of level walking, then climb again. The trail is rough and steep from here, and you'll be convinced you're hiking up the middle of a creekbed, especially if you get wet feet. Watch for goldenrod, spiraea, lupine, and pearly everlasting among the rocks.

The grade levels off at 2.7 miles, and you'll enter the shade of lodgepole pines, western white pines, and mountain hemlocks. Alas, the climb resumes too soon. Ascend through trees, then labor steeply up through rocks again until you hit the ridgetop at 3.1 miles. Savor easier going from here.

Pick your way through a slide area scarred with a lot of toppled trees at the 3.6-mile point, then begin to climb once more. Be sure to keep an eye out for a small sign on a tree to the left of the trail not long afterward. It points out the short spur trail to Tyler's Grave.

Tyler's Grave is marked by a small, marble headstone and a pile of rocks, overgrown with a spray of mountain heather. According to tradition, the unfortunate Tyler was a ranch hand who perished in a snowstorm in 1882.

Continue with the main trail, marked by ducks and blazes, and watch for the waters of Gertrude Lake off to the left. Angle over to gain the lakeshore at 4.1 miles.

Gertrude Lake is small but deep enough for swimming, with a low wall of granite on one side and numerous western white pines dropping shade along the shore. There are scores of flat rocks for sunbathing or snoozes, and if you're lucky, you'll have the place all to yourself.

You can explore the surrounding canyon, peppered with a handful of pothole lakes, or cut over to see Tyler Lake, a short distance away. Enjoy the solitude of Gertrude Lake awhile, then turn back toward your starting point.

● ● ● ● ● ● ● ● ● ● ● ● ● ● ● ● ● ● ● ● ● ● ● ● ●

# 62   RALSTON LAKE

Distance: 8.8 miles round trip
Difficulty: Moderate
Starting point: 7,420 feet
High point: 7,880 feet
Map: USGS Echo Lake 7.5'

The Echo Lake area off Highway 50 is extremely popular with day hikers (day-use permits are required), backpackers, and fishermen. If at all possible, visit on a weekday. You'll appreciate the region's startling scenic beauty much more if you can mix in a bit of solitude with the views.

This hike to Ralston Lake is a good sampler of the riches to be found along the Echo Lake Trail. If you find the 8.8-mile round-trip total somewhat daunting, you can cut 2.7 miles from your journey by taking the water taxi one way along Echo Lake. This is a good shortcut, and it opens up additional day-hike possibilities in this scenic, lake-dotted canyon. The ride will set you back a bit, however. One-way cost in 1988 was $5.50 for adults, $3.50 for children.

To reach the trailhead for Ralston Lake, drive 1.0 mile west of Echo Summit (or 7.9 miles east of Strawberry) on Highway 50, and turn north for Echo Lake. Drive the paved road 0.6 mile, then go left, continuing another 0.9 mile to the Echo Lake parking lot. The Echo Lake Chalet is 0.2 mile farther on, but its lot has a 2-hour parking limit.

From the upper parking lot, take the footpath down the hill (it starts across the road and just to the right of a green gas storage tank) toward the lakeshore. Arrive at the Echo Lake boat launch at 0.2 mile, where a water taxi makes regular departures.

If you're doing this trek solely on "sole power," cross the lower end of Echo Lake on the dam, and pause for a fine view out across the water toward a handful of distant peaks. Leave the dam and climb away from the water with the trail. Watch for an overlook spot to the right just before the trail veers left along Echo Lake's shoreline. You'll have a nice vista of Lake Tahoe from here.

Continue your trek above the shore of Echo Lake on a level, well-maintained trail. Walk a hillside decorated with manzanita, canyon live oak, sulfur flower, and nude buckwheat. Occasional Sierra junipers and Jeffrey pines offer shade, and you can gaze down on the many luxurious vacation cabins strung out along the shore as you hike toward the far end of the lake.

Look for the form of Pyramid Peak above the water, and pick

up views of Ralston Peak (Hike 63) to its left as you continue. You'll hit a pair of switchbacks and climb gently at 1.3 miles, then descend gradually as you near the end of Echo Lake at 2.0 miles. The trail leads on to parallel the shore of Upper Echo Lake (this is actually all one lake, joined by a narrow channel of water).

Pace a rocky, open hillside for a while, then enter a lodgepole pine forest with a lot of lupine and mountain pennyroyal. You'll be joined by a trail ascending from the water taxi dropoff spot at 2.8 miles. Continue straight and draw away from Echo Lake.

Climb gently on a rocky trail, and reach an entry sign for the Desolation Wilderness at 3.1 miles. There is a fine view back toward Echo Lake from the hillside. The ascent is moderate but steady as you proceed to a junction for Tamarack Lake at 3.9 miles. Go left here, abandoning the main trail leading on toward Lake of the Woods and Lake Aloha.

Follow the sometimes faint side trail toward Tamarack Lake, using ducks to find your way across a granite-sprinkled hilltop. Soon after, a view of Tamarack Lake appears to the right. Angle right to reach the lakeshore at 4.1 miles.

Tamarack Lake is large and deep, with a pine-shaded shoreline and a lot of oft-used campspots. Ralston Peak dominates the view above the south side of the lake. Skirt to the left along the shore to continue on toward Ralston Lake.

Cross the outlet creek from Tamarack Lake, and gain a use trail leading on toward Ralston Lake. Keep a sharp eye out for ducks that mark the way. Climb a low granite mound at 4.3 miles, and get your first look down onto Ralston Lake. A short descent leads to the shore at 4.4 miles.

Rocky little Ralston Lake is snuggled right into the base of bulky Ralston Peak. Deep, cold, and crystal clear, Ralston Lake has a lovely, stark setting that will make you glad you made the journey. Its waters are tempting to both swimmers and fishermen, whereas picnickers may be content to simply take off their boots and soak in the view.

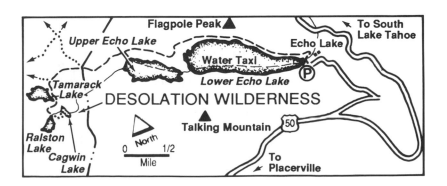

*The Ralston Peak hike is rich in scenic beauty.*

• • • • • • • • • • • • • • • • • • • • • • • • •

# 63  RALSTON PEAK

Distance: 8.0 miles round trip
Difficulty: Strenuous
Starting point: 6,420 feet
High point: 9,240 feet
Map: USGS Echo Lake 7.5'

If you're looking for a challenging hike with a big reward at the finish, try this demanding ascent to the summit of Ralston Peak. Start early in the day to beat the heat, and time your trek for clear weather to gain the full benefit of the view. Be sure to carry a windbreaker and a lot of water, and don't forget a day-hike permit, too.

To reach the trailhead for Ralston Peak, drive 3.2 miles east of Strawberry (or 5.7 miles west of Echo Summit) on Highway 50. Park on the north side of the road, just across from Camp Sacramento. A sign at the trailhead identifies the Ralston Trail.

Start uphill on the paved road that takes off to the right from the parking area (don't veer off onto the steep dirt road that branches to the left). Continue on pavement for about 0.2 mile, then approach the signed Ralston Trail, a dirt path that exits to the left from the paved route.

Begin climbing through a forest of white firs, red firs, and Jeffrey pines. The grade is moderate and sometimes steep, but always unrelenting. If the day is warm and sunny, you'll be glad for the shade of the abundant trees as you ascend.

Keep to the right as the trail branches at 0.6 mile, then enjoy a brief, level stretch at the 0.8-mile point. Resume climbing much too soon. The forest opens up a bit as you continue, and you'll gain a view out over the canyon from a manzanita-covered ridge at 1.2 miles.

Continue up through trees, watching for nude buckwheat and scores of ferns on the forest floor. The grade intensifies soon afterward, climbing steeply to a small wilderness sign denoting the boundary of the Desolation Wilderness at 1.6 miles.

Keep on climbing, with views across the canyon to the Sierra Ski Ranch. Mountain hemlocks and manzanita line the trail as you continue steeply up. At 1.7 miles, there's a view spot to the left of the trail. To the west, you'll spot Pyramid Peak from here.

Climb through a rocky, open landscape as you continue a punishing ascent. The trail becomes extremely steep from here, and thick underbrush threatens to overwhelm the often indistinct path. Fight your way upward through canyon live oak, pinemat manzanita, chinquapin, and brambles. As the brush closes in, the views expand.

You'll breathe a sigh of relief as you gain a lupine-dotted ridgetop at 2.6 miles. Savor a brief break as you skirt along a hillside decorated with mountain pennyroyal and sulfur flower, and drink in dramatic views of Pyramid Peak. Alas, the punishment resumes at 2.9 miles as you turn into the hill again.

Endure a steady up across a meadowy hilltop. The beauty of the early-season wildflowers will dull your pain a bit. You'll gain a ridgetop at 3.4 miles. A second trail joins in from Echo Lake up here, but you must descend a little to hit this more-defined route to Ralston Peak's summit.

For the most direct summit assault, leave the trail at the crest of the ridgetop (before it goes downhill to hook up with the Echo Lake route). Angle right and utilize faint use paths marked with scattered ducks to follow the ridgeline up to the summit of Ralston Peak. (Note: if you veer left instead of right from the trail, a 0.2-mile detour will take you to a spectacular viewspot above Ropi Lake, Lake of the Woods, and Lake Aloha, with Lake Tahoe in the distance. It's worth it!)

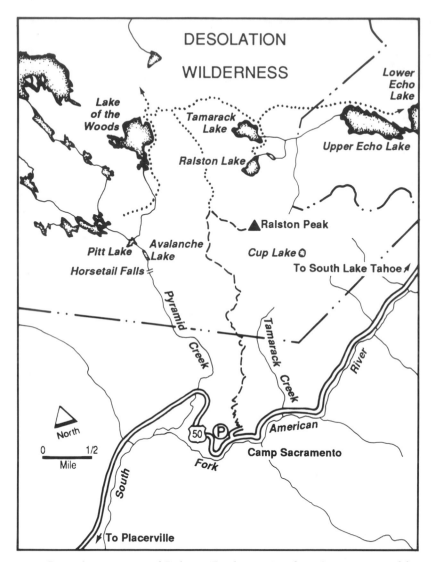

Gain the summit of Ralston Peak at 4.0 miles. As you scramble up a final barren expanse of loose rock, you'll feel like you're on a mountaintop at last. This rugged little summit commands a fantastic view in all directions. Pull up a rock, pull out a picnic, and enjoy the sights.

You'll see Round Top (Hike 51) to the south off Carson Pass, Echo Lake to the east, and Fallen Leaf Lake and glistening Lake Tahoe to the north. And just below you'll see Ralston Lake (Hike 62) and Tamarack Lake. This is a view you won't soon forget—and a climb your legs will hold against you for many days to come.

• • • • • • • • • • • • • • • • • • • • • • • • •

# 64   DARDANELLES LAKE

Distance: 7.2 miles round trip
Difficulty: Moderate
Starting point: 7,270 feet
High point: 8,080 feet
Total climb: 1,460 feet
Maps: USGS Echo Lake 7.5' and USGS Freel Peak 7.5'

This pleasant hike to Dardanelles Lake is perfect for a family day-hike destination. It's not too long, not too tough, and not too far off the beaten track, but it's chock full of quiet forest walking, wonderful wildflowers, and opportunities for unlimited lakeside lounging.

To reach the trailhead for Dardanelles Lake, drive south on Highway 89, proceeding 5.0 miles from its junction with Highway 50. Watch for a large parking area on the north side of the road. This is a popular trailhead, and the lot is often full on weekends; however, there is talk of putting in a new trailhead parking lot within the next few years.

Leave your vehicle, and carefully cross Highway 89 to reach the trailhead on the south side of the road. A sign identifies the route for Round Lake and Big Meadow. Start out climbing right away, ascending through a forest of red firs, Jeffrey pines, and lodgepole pines.

Pass through a gap in a barbed-wire fence at 0.3 mile. Breathe easier as the grade begins to mellow, and emerge into Big Meadow at 0.5 mile. This broad, grassy basin is home to battalions of bovines in late summer, so come early if you hope to see the wildflowers.

Cross a creek on a fancy wooden footbridge as you start across the meadow. At 0.8 mile, you'll regain the trees, then resume climbing at a moderate but steady incline. The trail is lined with lupine and aster, thriving in the partial shade of white and red firs.

The forest opens up a bit at 1.2 miles, and sage and mule ears take over where the lupine leaves off. Watch for scattered Sierra junipers, too. Continue uphill and come in beside a smaller meadow at 1.7 miles. The climb eases briefly here. Cross a fenceline and reach the crest of the hill (1.9-mile point).

Enjoy a steady descent through trees and arrive at the turnoff trail for Round Lake at 2.1 miles. (It's 0.7 mile to Round Lake from the junction.) Go right for Christmas Valley here, then descend through red firs and quaking aspens. You'll reach an unsigned trail junction at 2.3 miles. Keep to the left to continue toward Dardanelles Lake.

*Hikers pace the path to Dardanelles Lake.*

Cross a stream awash in Indian paintbrush, lupine, and monkey-flower. A second stream demands a shaky log crossing, then enjoy level walking past a lily-sprinkled pond. Start gently down beside Round Lake's outlet stream, admiring several handsome old junipers along the way.

You'll cross the stream on another log at 3.2 miles, then begin climbing as you leave the water. Work your way uphill through a granite-studded landscape, and arrive at sprawling Dardanelles Lake at 3.6 miles.

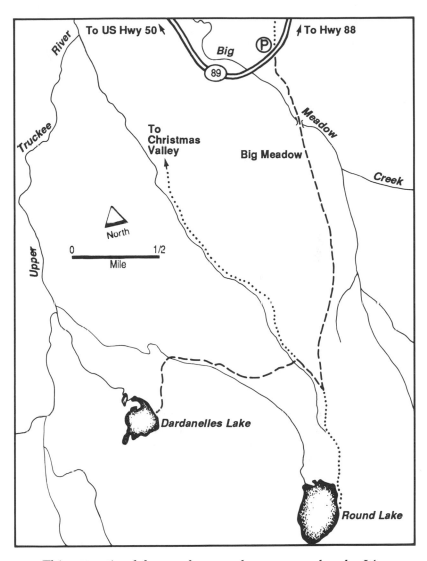

This attractive lake can be very busy on weekends. It's easy to see why—Dardanelles Lake is wonderfully scenic. One end is hemmed in by sheer granite cliffs, whereas lodgepole pines and mountain hemlocks decorate much of the remaining shoreline. Picnicking and swimming spots abound, and fishermen will find lots of places to plunk in their fishing lines.

Simply retrace your steps to regain your starting point, adding in the 1.4-mile round-trip jog to Round Lake if you have the time and energy. It's not as attractive as Dardanelles Lake, but the trail winds through an interesting landscape along the way.

# CHAPTER NINE

• • • • • • • • •

# Lake Tahoe/Donner Pass (Highway 89/Interstate 80)

Expect to have a lot of company on all of the hikes around Lake Tahoe and Donner Pass. The crowds can't be helped. People flock to the captivating Lake Tahoe like moths to a flame. And who can blame them? Even so, if you're able to go a bit beyond the beaten tourist track, and if you make a point of avoiding weekend hiking whenever possible, you'll find an abundance of enchanting destinations in the area.

Currently, all trails under the jurisdiction of the Lake Tahoe Basin Management Unit require day-hiking permits (this applies to Hikes 65–71). No quota system is in effect at present, although there has been talk of establishing limits on day use in the future. Many trailheads offer self-issue permits on-site, but it's a good idea to pick up your permit in advance (and check on changes in regulations at the same time).

Day-hike permits are available at the Lake Tahoe Visitors Information Center, just off Highway 89, 3.1 miles west of its junction with Highway 50. This is a great spot to gather campground information, purchase maps and guidebooks, etc. Permits are also issued at the Lake Tahoe Basin Management Unit, PO Box 731002, 870 Emerald Bay Road, South Lake Tahoe, California 95731.

Trails in this area provide access to the Desolation Wilderness (refer to chapter 8 for background information) and to the Granite Chief Wilderness.

One word of warning if you're planning to do some camping while you hike—the Tahoe/Donner Pass campgrounds are often full to overflowing. If you want to stay at a state park campground or at one of the more developed Forest Service sites, you'll probably need reservations. These can be obtained through Ticketron or the Forest Service's (800) 280-CAMP number.

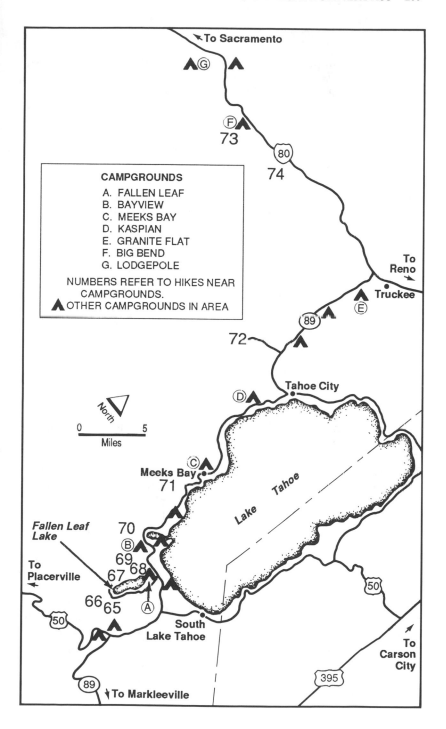

To Sacramento

G

F
73

80
74

CAMPGROUNDS
A. FALLEN LEAF
B. BAYVIEW
C. MEEKS BAY
D. KASPIAN
E. GRANITE FLAT
F. BIG BEND
G. LODGEPOLE

NUMBERS REFER TO HIKES NEAR
CAMPGROUNDS.
OTHER CAMPGROUNDS IN AREA

To
Reno

Truckee
E

89

72

Tahoe City

D

North

0        5
Miles

Lake  Tahoe

Meeks Bay
C
71

Fallen Leaf
Lake

70

B
69
68
67

To
Placerville

66 65

A

50

South
Lake Tahoe

To
Carson
City

50

89

To Markleeville

395

# CAMPGROUNDS

**Fallen Leaf Campground** *(Hike 65, Grass Lake; Hike 66, Susie and Heather lakes; Hike 67, Mount Tallac)*   This huge campground near busy Fallen Leaf Lake provides good access to several hikes, but you'll undoubtedly need reservations for a weekend site (contact Ticketron). To find Fallen Leaf Campground, drive 0.9 mile east of the Baldwin Beach turnoff on Highway 89, and take the road signed for Fallen Leaf Lake. Drive this paved road 0.5 mile to the campground entrance.

The 200 roomy, shaded campsites for tents or motorhomes boast picnic tables, fireplaces, and drinking water, and flush toilets are available. Fallen Leaf Campground is open May through October. Reservations accepted. Moderate fee.

**Bayview Campground** *(Hike 68, Cascade Falls; Hike 69, Granite Lake; Hike 70, Eagle and Middle Velma lakes)*   Oft-overlooked Bayview Campground is a wonderful option for the reservationless Tahoe camper. The trailheads for Hikes 68 and 69 leave right from the campground, and you can walk to Inspiration Point Vista above Emerald Bay from here.

No visitor to the Lake Tahoe area can help but be awed by their first glimpse of enchanting Emerald Bay. This is a truly beautiful body of water, whittled out by glaciers more skillful than the hand of a master carver. The characteristic Tahoe blue makes the bay unforgettable, as does the presence of rocky Fannette Island, plunked down in the center. You'll get your best view of Emerald Bay from Inspiration Point Vista, just across Highway 89 from Bayview Campground.

To find the campground, turn off Highway 89 at the sign for Bayview Campground (just opposite Inspiration Point Vista). If you're coming from the south, look for the turnoff at the crest of your climb from Baldwin Beach. Fifteen shaded tentspots have picnic tables, fireplaces, and non-flush toilets, but there is no drinking water available. Be forewarned, there is a one-night limit for this little campground.

Bayview Campground is open June through September. No reservations. No fee.

**Meeks Bay Campground** *Hike 70, Eagle and Middle Velma lakes; Hike 71, Crag Lake)*   This sprawling campground doesn't have much in the way of atmosphere. It's too close to Highway 89, and sites are rather barren and shadeless. It does provide access to the Tahoe shoreline, however, and that can be a rarity along this heavily developed stretch of real estate.

To find the campground, drive Highway 89 to just south of

Tahoma or just north of Rubicon Bay to a sign for the Meeks Bay Resort. Come early if you want to be assured of a weekend spot. The campground's 40 sites for tents or motorhomes offer picnic tables, fireplaces, drinking water, and flush toilets. Meeks Bay Campground is open June through September. No reservations. Moderate fee.

**Kaspian Campground** *(Hike 70, Eagle and Middle Velma lakes; Hike 71, Crag Lake)* Little Kaspian Campground is a charmer—inexpensive, uncrowded, and within walking distance of Lake Tahoe's sparkling water. There is one drawback, however; shaded hillside sites require a short walk in from the paved parking area. You'll need a tent and strong arms to stay here.

To find the 10 tentspots at Kaspian Campground, drive Highway 89 to just north of Tahoe Pines or just south of Ward Creek State Park, and watch for a sign for Kaspian Campground/Picnic Area. The campground is on the west side of Highway 89.

Sites offer picnic tables, fireplaces, drinking water, and flush toilets. Kaspian Campground is open June through September. No reservations. Minimal fee.

**Granite Flat Campground** *(Hike 71, Crag Lake; Hike 72, Five Lakes)* Set on the chortling Truckee River, Granite Flat Campground is popular with fishermen and recreational vehicle long-termers. The primitive sites lack drinking water, but fireplaces, picnic tables, and non-flush toilets are available.

You'll have to put up with quite a bit of road noise from Highway 89 if you claim one of the 70-plus spots for tents or motorhomes, and the shadeless sites can be toasty on a sunny summer day. But the Truckee River will be right in your backyard, if you want to escape the heat with a little toe wiggling.

To find the campground, drive Highway 89 to 6.8 miles north of the Squaw Valley turnoff or 1.5 miles south of the I-80 junction. Granite Flat Campground is open April through October. No reservations. No fee.

**Big Bend Campground** *(Hike 73, Loch Leven Lakes)* Set next to the Big Bend Visitor Information Center, the Big Bend Campground is a pleasant spot on the Yuba River. The one drawback of this attractive Forest Service campground is the constant hum of traffic emanating from the I-80 Freeway.

More than a dozen shaded sites for tents or motorhomes offer picnic tables, fireplaces, non-flush toilets, and drinking water. To find Big Bend Campground, turn off the I-80 Freeway at the Big Bend exit, and follow signs to the campground. No reservations. Moderate fee.

*The trail to Grass Lake appeals to hikers of all abilities.*

**Lodgepole Campground** *(Hike 74, Long Lake)* This midsized Pacific Gas & Electric campground is a pleasant spot to pass a few idyllic days. Its 18 sites for tents or motorhomes are quiet and shaded, and the campground is near the Lake Valley Reservoir, where fishermen can ply their trade.

To find the campground, turn off the I-80 Freeway at the Yuba Gap exit, and drive 2.0 miles (0.3 of it on unpaved road), following signs for Lodgepole Campground. Sites offer picnic tables, fireplaces, non-flush toilets, and drinking water. Lodgepole Campground is open May through September. No reservations. Moderate fee.

## 65 GRASS LAKE

Distance: 5.4 miles round trip
Difficulty: Easy
Starting point: 6,720 feet
High point: 7,240 feet
Maps: USGS Echo Lake 7.5' and USGS Emerald Bay 7.5'

This pleasant, easy hike makes an excellent family excursion. It offers a scenic lake destination, without the challenging climb some of the other Tahoe-area treks demand. The trailhead that provides access to Grass Lake, as well as Susie and Heather lakes (Hike 66), is extremely popular, however, so try to avoid visiting on a weekend.

To reach the trailhead for Grass Lake, drive Highway 89 to 0.9 miles east of the Baldwin Beach turnoff, and take the road signed for Fallen Leaf Lake. Drive the paved road past Fallen Leaf Campground, keep right at the first junction, then go left for Desolation Trails at the second junction. You'll go left once more just before a bridge across Glen Alpine Creek.

The road deteriorates from here. Cross a bridge at the end of Lily Lake, and reach a very limited parking area 5.6 miles from Highway 89. A sign at the spot proclaims this the Glen Alpine trailhead. Self-issue day hike permits were available here in 1989.

Set off on the rocky road leading from the parking area (don't take the old fire road), and walk in the shade of willows, quaking aspens, and white firs. At 0.3 mile there is a gate and a sign denoting

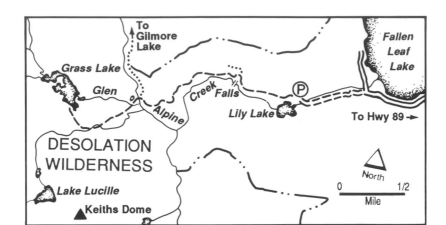

this as a private road. Continue with your exceedingly rocky route.

Keep to the right at the junction that follows, and climb gently beside Glen Alpine Creek. There's a small waterfall at the 0.5-mile point, and you'll spot a lot of private cabins strung out along the way. Continue climbing from the waterfall, and keep left at the next junction.

The road levels out at 0.7 mile as you hike through manzanita, canyon live oak, and scattered Jeffrey pines. Watch for evidence of beaver activity along the creek. The cabins will accompany you until the extremely rough road ends (mercifully) at 1.2 miles. Look for a signpost for Gilmore, Susie, and Grass lakes here.

Climb on a moderately graded trail through lodgepole pines, Jeffrey pines, and white firs, then ascend more noticeably as you enter an open landscape sprinkled with tough Sierra junipers. You'll reach an entry sign for the Desolation Wilderness at 1.6 miles. A signed trail junction follows shortly afterward.

Go left for Grass Lake, cross Gilmore Lake's outlet creek, and climb very gently to passs a small pond at 1.9 miles. Next cross Glen Alpine Creek (Grass Lake's outlet), then ascend through an open granite landscape brightened with the blossoms of spiraea. The grade intensifies as you scramble up through the rocks.

Gain more level walking at 2.4 miles, and stroll onward to arrive at the shore of spacious Grass Lake at 2.7 miles. If you're hiking early in the year, you'll be treated to the sight of a lovely waterfall descending toward Grass Lake from Susie Lake's outlet point (Hike 66).

Later in the summer, tempting swimming opportunities abound along Grass Lake's rocky shore, or you can enjoy a picnic in the shade of the scattered western white pines or mountain hemlocks that line the water. Be sure to look for Jacks Peak and Dicks Peak above the lake's west end.

# 66   SUSIE AND HEATHER LAKES

Distance: 10.6 miles round trip
Difficulty: Strenuous
Starting point: 6,720 feet
High point: 7,960
Maps: USGS Echo Lake 7.5', USGS Emerald Bay 7.5',
    and USGS Rockbound Valley 7.5'

Because of its distance and the climb involved, this hike to Susie and Heather lakes makes for a challenging one-day trip. However, both Susie and Heather lakes are well worth the journey. One word of encouragement—if you make it as far as Susie Lake and feel like turning back, do try to summon the energy to walk the extra mile to Heather Lake. There are few lakes more scenic than this one in all of the Sierra.

The hike to Susie and Heather lakes shares its trailhead and the first 1.7 miles of walking with the trek to Grass Lake. Read the first seven paragraphs of Hike 65 to get you on your way.

*Heather Lake's rocky shoreline is a gem of stark Sierra loveliness.*

From the junction just beyond the Desolation Wilderness entry sign, go straight for Dicks Pass, and continue ascending beside Glen Alpine Creek. The terrain is mostly rocky and open, although scattered Sierra junipers and Jeffrey pines provide occasional shade. Climb steadily, with fine views of the surrounding ridges.

Cross Gilmore Lake's outlet creek at 3.3 miles, then arrive at a junction just afterward. The trail to the right leads to Gilmore Lake. Go left to continue on for Susie and Heather lakes (the sign calls out Lake Aloha). Enjoy level walking as you pass a series of small ponds, then begin descending steadily at 3.5 miles.

Reach another junction and the end of your downhill hiking at 3.8 miles. Continue to the left toward Susie and Heather lakes (signed for Lake Aloha). Slosh through a marshy area brightened with a plethora of wildflowers, and look for narrow goldenrod, cow parsnip, Indian paintbrush, lupine, and swamp onion as you cross a seasonal stream, then begin to climb.

Ascend steadily to the 4.1-mile point. You'll see Susie Lake just ahead as you reach the crest of your climb. Press on to reach the shore of this large, deep lake at 4.2 miles. With a curving shore and a center sprinkled with picturesque granite islands, Susie Lake is a scenic spot to take a break.

When you're ready to move on, swing left with the trail along the shore, and cross Susie Lake's outlet stream at 4.4 miles. (Your feet may get wet early in the season.) A use trail departs to the left just afterward. This short detour leads to several nice campspots and a great overlook of Grass Lake.

Continue with the main trail along Susie Lake's shoreline, enjoying the company of mountain heather and spiraea. Turn away from the lake at 4.8 miles, and begin the moderate climb toward Heather Lake. Be sure to pause for a glance back at the handsome picture made by Susie Lake.

Gain more level walking after about 0.2 mile, and wind onward through a desolate landscape of rock and junipers and stunted

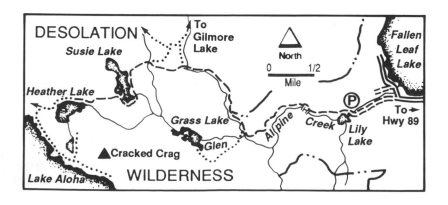

pines. The harshness of the scene adds to its lonely beauty. Arrive at spectacularly situated Heather Lake at 5.3 miles. You'll be glad you came.

Heather Lake lies in a world of granite. Its shoreline is rock, and rock dominates its scenery. Look for rugged Mount Price and pointed Pyramid Peak from the trail along the north shore of the lake, and gaze up toward the far end of the lake to see the beckoning pass toward Lake Aloha, a favorite destination of backpackers.

Heather Lake is deep and cold—too cold for any but the heartiest of swimmers. But picnickers can soak in the unforgettable scenery for as long as they desire. Linger long and drink your fill of this starkly beautiful corner of the Sierra.

● ● ● ● ● ● ● ● ● ● ● ● ● ● ● ● ● ● ● ● ● ● ● ●

# 67 MOUNT TALLAC

Distance: 10.0 miles round trip
Difficulty: Strenuous
Starting point: 6,400 feet
High point: 9,740 feet
Map: USGS Emerald Bay 7.5'

This hike to the summit of Mount Tallac isn't easy. In fact, the climb is downright punishing much of the way. Don't try it if you're not in shape. Don't try it if you're afraid of heights. And don't try it on a cloudy day. But if you're willing to work hard, and if you've got an entire day to spend, and if you want to earn the most spectacular view of Lake Tahoe anyone could ever hope to see, don't miss this hike. It's a winner!

To find the trail for Mount Tallac, drive 0.7 mile north of the Lake Tahoe Visitors Information Center on Highway 89, and turn left onto a paved road signed for the Mount Tallac trailhead. Drive 0.3 mile to a junction and keep left, then lose the pavement 0.2 mile later. Reach the trailhead parking area 1.1 miles from Highway 89.

Begin walking at the trailhead information board, setting out on an old roadbed lined with sage and overhung by massive Jeffrey pines. At 0.1 mile, keep to the right for Mount Tallac, and begin climbing on a rocky trail with the bulk of Mount Tallac straight ahead.

The forest floor is overrun with manzanita and canyon live oak as you continue, and patches of mule ears add their bright yellow blossoms to the overwhelming green. A steady climb eases at 0.6 mile, but the ascent resumes soon after as you gain a fine view down to Fallen Leaf Lake and out to Lake Tahoe in the distance.

Follow an exceedingly rocky ridgetop trail with Fallen Leaf Lake to the left and Mount Tallac to the right, climbing gently beneath white firs and Jeffrey pines. Abandon the ridgetop at 1.2 miles. A brief descent becomes a steady climb as you angle toward the base of Mount Tallac.

Hike through a shady white fir forest, and reach an entry sign for the Desolation Wilderness at 1.7 miles. Pretty little Floating Island Lake appears soon afterward. The lake's lush shoreline is a nice spot for a breather, awash in labrador tea and bright spiraea. But don't linger too long—you've got a long climb ahead.

Abandon Floating Island Lake, and ascend past an abundance of wildflowers as you enter more open terrain. Watch for crimson columbine, false Solomon's seal, and angelica as you climb beside a rocky creekbed. A little knoll yields another view of Lake Tahoe at 2.3 miles.

Descend to cross Cathedral Creek at 2.4 miles, and climb to a trail junction just beyond. Keep right here for Cathedral Lake. Another bout of climbing leads to the rocky shore of petite Cathedral Lake at 2.6 miles. Now the real grunt begins.

"Steep" takes on a new definition as you leave Cathedral Lake. Ascend dramatically on a shadeless, rocky trail, lined with pinemat manzanita. The footing is awful, the sun is hot, and the grade is torturous—but the views are increasingly magnificent. Pause to gasp for breath while you enjoy them.

The unrelenting up intensifies at 3.3 miles. Gaze ahead and you'll see your trail shooting up toward the ridgetop. Things look

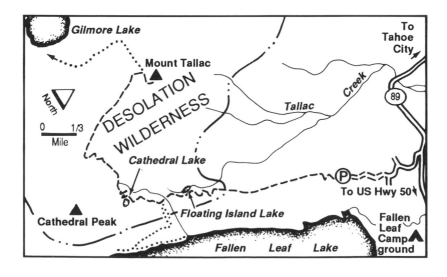

*Young hikers reach the summit of 9,740-foot Mount Tallac.*

pretty gruesome here. Console yourself with promises of the summit vista, and look for snatches of bright spiraea, mountain pennyroyal, rockfringe, and mountain heather to cheer you as you climb.

You'll reach a junction at 3.4 miles where a use trail (unofficially signed "Hard Way") takes off to the right. This route is shorter but more difficult. Keep to the main route and gain the ridgetop at 3.5 miles. Wow! Your energy level will soar as you savor an outstanding view of the peaks to the south. Look for Pyramid Peak and Ralston Peak (Hike 63) in the distance.

Enjoy easier walking as you swing around the hillside for your assault on the summit. If the day is breezy, the wind can be downright fierce right here. Your climb resumes in earnest at 3.8 miles, but you'll pick up more and more peaks on the horizon as you gain elevation.

Ascend through wildflower meadows overrun with blossoms in early season, and watch for stunted whitebark pines and stout western white pines sprinkled across the slopes. You'll get a disheartening view of your final goal at 4.1 miles as you gain sight of the summit. It still looks much too far away.

Continue climbing with a vista of the Susie/Heather lakes basin

(Hike 66), and pick up a view of Gilmore Lake as you hike on amid an amazing profusion of wildflowers. Look for Sierra arnica, California corn lily, little elephant heads, yarrow, fireweed, and sulfur flower as you go.

Reach a junction with the trail from Gilmore Lake at 4.7 miles, and go right to continue your ascent on a rocky pathway marked with ducks. You'll regain your view of Lake Tahoe at 4.9 miles as you emerge onto an exposed ridge that will make you feel as though you're walking a tightrope strung above the world.

The trail is indistinct from here; just continue up. Gain the 9,740-foot summit of Mount Tallac at 5.0 miles. The view is simply awesome. This barren patch of rocks provides a 360-degree panorama that you'll never forget.

Vast and dazzlingly blue Lake Tahoe rules the scene, with Emerald Bay a major landmark, but the peaks to the south are enchanting, too. And you'll see lakes everywhere. The Desolation Wilderness looks anything but desolate from here. Pull out a map to help you in your identification efforts, and pull out a sandwich to replenish some of the energy the hill sucked out of you. Then simply lean back and enjoy.

## 68   CASCADE FALLS

Distance: 1.5 miles round trip
Difficulty: Easy
Starting point: 6,900 feet
High point: 6,920 feet
Total climb: 400 feet
Map: USGS Emerald Bay 7.5'

*Jeffrey pinecone*

This short, effortless hike to Cascade Falls presents a good opportunity to burn off a little energy in the middle of a day of driving or sightseeing. Or combine the walk with the trek to Granite Lake that leaves from the same trailhead, and make a two-hike day of it. Cascade Falls is a super family outing, but please be careful with young children, as there are several exposed dropoffs and the falls can be dangerous.

To reach the trailhead for Cascade Falls, turn off Highway 89 at the Bayview Campground (just opposite Inspiration Point Vista above Emerald Bay). Drive through the campground and find a hikers' parking lot at the far end of the road. If the lot is full, you can leave your car at the vista parking area across Highway 89 (add 0.4 mile round trip to your walk).

From the hikers' parking lot, set out on the trail to the left, signed for Cascade Falls. Pace a dusty route through a forest of Jeffrey pines and white firs, and keep to the right when the trail branches soon after you begin. If you're hiking in June, the sight of lovely bell-shaped blossoms on the manzanita bushes that line the way is a real treat.

Angle left at the second junction, and hike on to ascend a rocky knoll at the 0.2-mile point. From here, you'll have a wonderful view out to Lake Tahoe and down to Cascade Lake. The views continue, and the roar of Cascade Falls becomes evident as you walk onward.

Look for Cascade Falls ahead as you round a bend in the trail soon afterward. This first vista is the nicest all-encompassing view

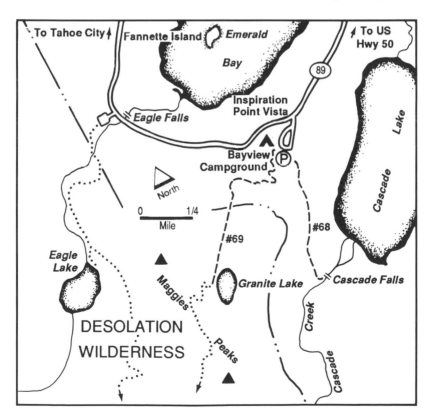

of the falls you'll get. The path of the glistening water across the stone is reminiscent of a horsetail shivering in the wind.

Begin a gentle descent on a very rocky path, then climb again as you reach the 0.6-mile point. Watch for shieldleaf, Indian paintbrush, and mountain pride penstemon along the rugged trail. Scramble across an open granite slope for the final 100 yards, then arrive at the edge of Cascade Falls at 0.7 mile.

One word of caution—be sure to note the spot where you reach the water's edge, as the trail can be difficult to locate when you turn back toward the parking area. Find a landmark and remember it.

Cascade Falls makes a wonderful short-hike destination. It's really a series of little waterfalls, a symphony of white water serenades, spilling over time-smoothed stone. This is a great picnic spot, and children will love the chatter of the water.

• • • • • • • • • • • • • • • • • • • • • • • • • •

# 69  GRANITE LAKE

Distance: 2.4 miles round trip
Difficulty: Moderate
Starting point: 6,800 feet
High point: 7,680 feet
Map: USGS Emerald Bay 7.5'

The trek to Granite Lake is a bit of a grunt. You climb and climb and climb to reach the lake. But the way is short, and the ascent is blessed with spectacular views of Lake Tahoe and Emerald Bay. If you have young children along, you should be able to lure them up the hill with the promise of a romp along the shore of Granite Lake. To reach the trailhead for Granite Lake, turn off Highway 89 at the Bayview Campground (just opposite Inspiration Point Vista above Emerald Bay). Drive through the campground and find a hikers' parking lot at the far end of the road. If the lot is full, leave your car at the vista parking area across Highway 89 (add 0.4 mile round trip to your walk).

Take the trail to the right, signed for Granite Lake and Dicks Lake, and begin climbing steadily beneath a white fir ceiling. The dusty path ascends unceasingly as you switchback up through a shady forest. As the trees begin to thin, catch glimpses of Lake Tahoe and Emerald Bay. Hold off on photos, though; the views get much better.

*Day hikers on trail from Granite Lake*

Reach an entry sign for the Desolation Wilderness at 0.5 mile. You'll cross a small stream and savor expanding views. Look for Cascade Lake below. Reach a boulder-cluttered viewpoint soon afterward. There's a wonderful vista of Emerald Bay, Lake Tahoe, and Fallen Leaf Lake from here.

Continue uphill to gain a second viewpoint (just as you round the bend). Keep a tight rein on children here, as the dropoff is precipitous. If you're weary from the unrelenting climb, this is the scenic highlight of the hike, so savor it and catch your breath.

Continue up more gently, walking through a red fir forest. The trail flattens out at 0.9 mile as you hike beside a creek, then begin to climb again. Come in above Granite Lake (to the left of trail), and abandon the main route to descend the hillside toward the lakeshore at 1.2 miles.

Granite Lake is small but attractive, with a rocky shoreline and some tempting dropoffs for would-be swimmers. Children will love exploring here, and weary parents can munch on sandwiches and console themselves with thoughts of the downhill backtrack to the car.

It is possible to connect this hike with the trek to Eagle Lake and Middle Velma Lake (Hike 70) by continuing on with the trail past Granite Lake; however, you'll need to consult a good area map and establish a short car shuttle.

• • • • • • • • • • • • • • • • • • • • • • • • •

# 70 EAGLE AND MIDDLE VELMA LAKES

Distance: 9.8 miles round trip
Difficulty: Strenuous
Starting point: 6,580 feet
High point: 8,230 feet
Total climb: 2,080 feet
Maps: USGS Emerald Bay 7.5' and USGS Rockbound Valley 7.5'

This hike to Middle Velma Lake is tough. There's no getting around it. And the trail is unpleasantly crowded for the first mile to Eagle Lake. Even so, the scenery will probably win you over. If it doesn't, maybe Middle Velma Lake's serene shoreline will.

Whatever you do, don't plan this trek for a weekend. The Forest Service counted 30,000 hikers here in a recent season. Most people stop at Eagle Lake, but that doesn't make parking any easier!

To reach the trailhead for Eagle and Middle Velma lakes, turn off Highway 89 at the sign for the Eagle Falls trailhead and picnic area. There are restrooms at the paved parking area. Self-issue day-hike permits were available here as of 1989.

Set out on a sandy trail, but exchange easy going for a steep and rocky climb soon afterward. Cross Eagle Creek on a deluxe footbridge at 0.2 mile, and continue ascending to reach an entry sign for the Desolation Wilderness 0.1 mile later.

Climb steeply beneath white firs and Jeffrey pines, and gain increasingly spectacular views down onto Emerald Bay. The incline mellows at 0.6 mile as you continue up in welcome white fir shade. The grade picks up again all too soon, and you'll puff uphill to the turnoff trail for Eagle Lake at 0.9 mile.

A short 0.1-mile jaunt leads to the shore of handsome Eagle Lake. If you don't feel like adding the 0.2-mile round trip to your total distance for the day, you can settle for a good view of Eagle Lake from the trail to Middle Velma Lake.

Eagle Lake is an amazingly crowded spot, reached by a terribly overworked trail. Where else in the Sierra Nevada can you see entire families hiking to a lake that's a mile from the road, carrying pop-laden coolers and portable barbecues? If you choose to visit Eagle Lake, pause a moment to admire the scenery (if you can see it through the people), then turn back to the main trail to press on toward Middle Velma Lake.

Lose the vast majority of your fellow hikers as you leave the junction and ascend along the hillside above Eagle Lake. Look for wildflowers nestled in the rocks along the trail, and watch for manzanita, bitter cherry, canyon live oak, and chinquapin.

Cross a seasonal stream at 1.3 miles, and climb steeply to reach an open expanse of granite 0.3 mile later. Watch for ducks as you work across this section; the trail is difficult to follow. Turn back to view your progress too. There's a spectacular vista of Eagle Lake and Lake Tahoe from here.

The ascent mellows briefly as you wind through a fern-carpeted forest, but it resumes with enthusiasm as you struggle upward to a saddle in the ridge at 2.1 miles. From here, look down onto the granite canyon beyond. Enjoy easier walking as you continue along the hillside.

The climb picks up again at 2.5 miles. The good news is that the bulk of the hill is behind you when you reach a trail junction at 2.8 miles. Go right here for Velma Lakes, and relish easy walking across a hilltop boasting western white pines, Jeffrey pines, and pinemat manzanita.

Gaze down into a stark granite canyon as you continue on a mostly level trail, and arrive at another junction at 3.6 miles. Keep right for Velma Lakes, and begin a snaking descent with views ahead to Middle Velma Lake. The steady downhill flattens out at 4.3 miles. Pass an unnamed (but lovely) lake shortly afterward, then cross a wide stream.

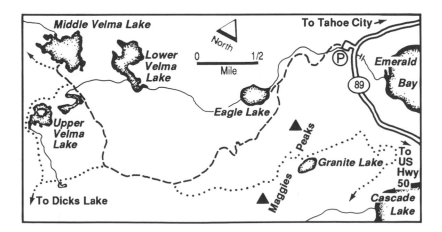

The junction with the trail to Upper Velma Lake appears at 4.7 miles. Continue straight for Middle Velma Lake, and climb gently to a second junction soon afterward. Stay straight again for Middle Velma Lake, then watch for the lake itself off to the right of the trail as you walk onward. You can leave the trail to scramble cross-country to the shore of Middle Velma Lake at 4.9 miles, or you can stay with the trail and reach the lakeshore farther on.

Middle Velma Lake is popular with backpackers, and it's easy to see why. The lake is long and deep, sprinkled with picturesque rocky islands. It offers a lot of tempting swimming spots, and fishermen seem to do quite well here. The scattered mountain hemlocks that decorate the granite shoreline provide shade for lazy lakeside picnics.

● ● ● ● ● ● ● ● ● ● ● ● ● ● ● ● ● ● ● ● ● ● ● ● ●

# 71  CRAG LAKE

Distance: 10.0 miles round trip
Difficulty: Moderate
Starting point: 6,240 feet
High point: 7,460 feet
Maps: USGS Homewood 7.5', USGS Meeks Bay 7.5',
    and USGS Rockbound Valley 7.5'

Despite the distance, this hike to Crag Lake really isn't tough. The ups are very mellow, and the shaded forest walking makes this a great hot-weather trek. The walk lacks the far-reaching vistas of some other Tahoe-area hikes, but it's not too crowded, and Crag Lake is a worthwhile destination.

To find the trailhead for Crag Lake, drive Highway 89 to the Meeks Bay Resort and claim a spot along the shoulder of the road. A bulletin board on the west side of Highway 89 proclaims this to be the Meeks Bay trailhead. Self-issue day-hike permits were available here as of 1989.

Start out on the sandy road to the right of the bulletin board (the road is closed off by a gate). Enjoy level walking for the first 1.3 miles of your trek as you tread a tree-shaded route lined with lupine, yarrow, fireweed, and narrow goldenrod. Look for lodgepole and Jeffrey pines, white firs, and incense cedars as you go.

Reach a signpost at 1.3 miles, and abandon the road and the Tahoe–Yosemite Trail to go right toward Crag Lake (signed for Phipps Pass). Begin climbing on a shaded trail, ascending steadily

*Trees and granite await the visitor to the Crag Lake trail.*

for 0.5 mile. You'll have gentle ups and downs to negotiate as you continue. Come in beside an alder-lined creek at 2.2 miles, and reach an entry sign for the Desolation Wilderness soon after.

Savor level walking through the trees as you hike onward, and look for lupine, spiraea, and bracken ferns on the forest floor. Arrive at a broad meadow at 2.5 miles and revel in the abundance of wildflowers here. Another climb begins a short time later. Ascend beside a singing stream, then cross it on a sturdy footbridge at the 3.5-mile point.

Climb gently once again, hiking in the cool shadows of red firs and lodgepole pines. Watch for an avalanche of thimbleberries as you ascend along a lush hillside. Then exchange shade for sunlight when you emerge onto an open, rocky slope, and continue steadily uphill above the stream.

Arrive on the forested shore of little Lake Genevieve at 4.6 miles. Keep to the left as the trail branches, following the sign for Phipps Pass to continue for Crag Lake. Walk a wide, sandy trail along the shore of Lake Genevieve, then resume climbing as you angle up toward your goal.

*Crag Lake boasts a scenic, boulder-strewn shoreline.*

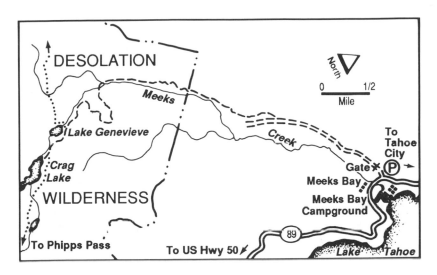

At 5.0 miles, reach the edge of Crag Lake. Crag Lake is much larger than Lake Genevieve, and it's prettier too. It boasts an attractive granite shoreline, deep waters to tempt swimmers and fishermen, and numerous campspots for visiting backpackers. Stroll the shore of Crag Lake, then pick your picnic spot and enjoy.

# 72 FIVE LAKES

Distance: 4.2 miles round trip
Difficulty: Moderate
Starting point: 6,560 feet
High point: 7,550 feet
Maps: USGS Granite Chief 7.5' and USGS Tahoe City 7.5'

Like the short hike to Eagle Lake (Hike 70), this brief trek to Five Lakes is a popular Tahoe trip. Unlike the Eagle Lake hike, however, this hike does not require a day-hike permit. Crowds are heavy on the weekends, so try to avoid Saturday and Sunday visits if you can. Even though it does involve a fairly steep climb, this is a neat family jaunt. The uphill is tolerable, and the lakes are fun to visit.

To find the Five Lakes trailhead, drive 3.8 miles northwest of Tahoe City (or 1.4 miles southeast of the Squaw Valley turnoff) on Highway 89, and turn onto the paved Alpine Meadows Road. Drive

2.1 miles to reach the trailhead parking strung out along the shoulder of the road. Watch your odometer when you turn off Highway 89, as there is no road sign to mark the spot.

Begin on a swiftly climbing path marked as the Five Lakes Trail. Ascend steadily along a hillside dotted with sage, canyon live oak, and manzanita, and gain a view over to the Alpine Meadows Ski Area as you climb. This trail is a good way to quickly discover what kind of shape you're in, as the uphill is unrelenting for the first 0.4 mile.

Puff onward through mountain pennyroyal, nude buckwheat, and mule ears, then enter increasingly rocky terrain as you negotiate a passel of switchbacks. There's virtually no shade throughout this climb, so you should be sweating up a storm by the time you reach the crest of the ridge at 1.2 miles.

Continue up at a moderate pace as you work upward along a rocky creek canyon. This rugged little canyon is a granite wonderland, and you'll decide that the wilderness area you're entering is aptly named when, at 1.6 miles, you arrive at a boundary sign for the Granite Chief Wilderness. The good news is that this marks the end of most of your climb.

Walk onward in the welcome shade of thick red firs, enjoying level walking as you continue toward Five Lakes. You'll pass a faint spur trail (to the left) leading down to the first of the lakes at 1.8 miles. Proceed to a signed junction at 1.9 miles, and go left here at the sign for Five Lakes.

Follow a level trail through trees and manzanita to arrive at the largest of the lakes at 2.1 miles. The lake isn't huge, but it's deep enough for swimming, with a tree-lined shore and an abundance of good rocks for sitting and sunbathing. Spread a picnic and pass the afternoon splashing or exploring.

# 73 LOCH LEVEN LAKES

Distance: 7.0 miles round trip
Difficulty: Moderate
Starting point: 5,720 feet
High point: 6,860 feet
Total climb: 1,390 feet
Maps: USGS Soda Springs 7.5' and
    USGS Cisco Grove 7.5'

*A fisherman follows the trail to
Loch Leven Lakes.*

This moderately challenging hike to Loch Leven Lakes is an excellent family outing, offering pleasant walking, lots of early wildflowers, and a trio of attractive lakes. You can make a shorter day of it by stopping at the first of the three Loch Leven Lakes, reached after only 2.2 miles.

To find the trailhead for Loch Leven Lakes, turn off the I-80 Freeway at the Big Bend exit and drive to the Big Bend Visitor Information Center (open dates depend on Forest Service funding). The trailhead is just to the west of the information center, on the south side of the road. Look for a sign for the Loch Leven Trail.

Begin by walking along a private road for 0.1 mile, then gain a signed trail ascending steadily past scores of wildflowers. Watch for mountain pride penstemon, single-stem groundsel, and Brewer's lupine as you climb. At 0.5 mile, you'll reach a vista point with views down onto the speeding vehicles on I-80.

Enjoy a brief level stretch as you continue, and trace the path of a lovely little creek awhile. Cross the waterway on a wooden footbridge, then resume climbing. Reach a set of railroad tracks at 0.8 mile, and cross carefully to regain the trail.

Ascend steadily on a shaded pathway lined with larkspur and numerous ferns, and enter a long series of switchbacks at 1.2 miles. The terrain opens up as you negotiate a rocky slope boasting canyon live oak and broadleaf lupine. A border of carefully placed stones designates the trail across the rock.

Reach the crest of your steep ascent at 1.8 miles, then continue up more gradually. You'll get your first look at Lower Loch Leven Lake at 2.1 miles, then drop steeply to reach the lakeshore at 2.2 miles. Lower Loch Leven Lake is a popular spot with backpackers, and it boasts an open shoreline paved with granite slabs.

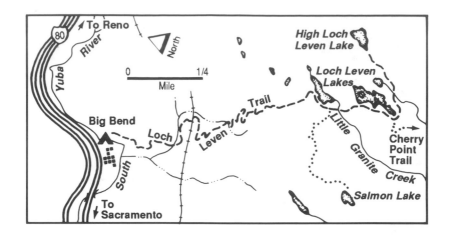

Continue with the trail along the shore, and reach a signed junction soon afterward. Go straight here for High Loch Leven Lake. The trail is difficult to follow as it winds through the rocky landscape beyond. It's best to keep to the higher route along the crest of the ridge.

You'll gain Middle Loch Leven Lake at 2.6 miles. This pretty little gem is sprinkled with tiny rock islands that make great spots

*High Loch Leven Lake is a treat for weary feet.*

for sunbathing. But don't stop now—there is one more lake to see. Wind along the lakeshore and reach a junction with the Cherry Point Trail at 2.8 miles; continue straight on the Loch Leven Trail.

Follow a string of orange-painted blazes through the rocks, and savor level walking for about 0.3 mile. The climb resumes at 3.2 miles, but the goal isn't far away now. Press on and up to reach the shore of High Loch Leven Lake at 3.5 miles.

You may have to share your picnic spot with the backpackers and fishermen that are attracted to this lovely lake, but that's okay—there's plenty of granite-covered shoreline for everyone. Linger at High Loch Leven for the remainder of your afternoon, or backtrack to one of the earlier lakes if you've picked a favorite.

• • • • • • • • • • • • • • • • • • • • • • • • •

# 74  LONG LAKE

Distance: 2.0 miles round trip
Difficulty: Easy
Starting point: 6,600 feet
High point: 6,730 feet
Map: USGS Soda Springs 7.5'

The hike to Long Lake is short but sweet, with plenty of pretty scenery and a pleasant destination. Plan a family outing, and bring a picnic and the fishing poles. Then simply enjoy.

To reach the trailhead for Long Lake, take the Soda Springs/Norden exit off the I-80 Freeway and drive south. Turn onto Soda Springs Road after 0.7 mile, then go right onto Pahatsi Road 0.9 mile later.

Lose the pavement after half a mile. Stay on the main route as you continue, ignoring spur roads to the left and right, and curve around the perimeter of Kidd Lake. Reach the Devil's Outlook Warming Hut and your stopping spot 3.9 miles from Soda Springs Road. (It's possible to drive another 0.3 mile to the trail's start, but the road is extremely rough from here.)

Leave your car and follow the road downhill, staying to the left at the junction. There is a view of 7,700-foot Devil's Peak as well as the twin Cascade Lakes on the left and right sides of the road. Reach the road's end at 0.3 mile, and continue down on a steep footpath.

Cross between the Cascade Lakes on a small dam, and arrive at a sign for the Palisade Creek Trail. Follow this level, lupine-lined trail through lodgepole pines as you hike to a junction at 0.7 mile.

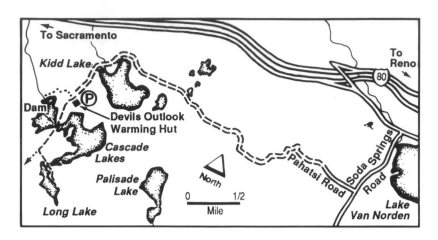

A trail to the right leads to the North Fork of the American River from here. Go left on the unsigned trail toward Long Lake.

Wind onward through a forest of white and red firs and lodgepole pines, and reach Long Lake at 0.8 mile. We've upped our one-way total to 1.0 mile, as you'll probably want to stroll on along Long Lake's pretty shoreline. Enjoy the fine view of Devil's Peak across the water. Long Lake is a wonderful short-hike destination, offering plenty of tempting picnic places and several good fishing and swimming spots.

•••••••••

# Further Reading

## VEGETATION

Horn, Elizabeth. *Wildflowers 3, the Sierra Nevada*. Beaverton, Oregon: Touchstone Press, 1976.

Little, Elbert L. *The Audubon Society Field Guide to North American Trees (Western Region)*. New York: Alfred A. Knopf, 1980.

Niehaus, Theodore. *Sierra Wildflowers, Mount Lassen to Kern Canyon*. Berkeley: University of California Press, 1974.

Spellenberg, Richard. *The Audubon Society Field Guide to North American Wildflowers*. New York: Alfred A. Knopf, 1979.

Wilson, Jim, Lynn Wilson, and Jeff Nichols. *Wildflowers of Yosemite*. Yosemite, California: Sunrise Productions, 1987.

## CAMPING

Stienstra, Tom. *California Camping, the Complete Guide to California's Recreation Areas*. San Francisco: Foghorn Press, 1987.

## YOSEMITE HISTORY

Farquhar, Francis P. *History of the Sierra Nevada*. Berkeley: University of California Press, 1965.

Muir, John. *The Yosemite*. New York: Doubleday, 1912.

# Index

• • • • • • • •

*Note: Bold face page numbers refer to photos*

*The authors savor the view from the summit of Ralston Peak.*

KAREN AND TERRY WHITEHILL live in Portland, Oregon. Avid outdoorspeople, they have cycled all over Europe and walked 4,000 miles from Paris to Jerusalem. They are the authors of other guidebooks, *Nature Walks In & Around Portland, Best Short Hikes in California's Southern Sierra, France by Bike* and *Europe by Bike* (The Mountaineers). They packed their 6-month-old daughter, Sierra Jo, to the top of Mount Whitney in the Sierra Nevada, while doing research for this guidebook.

*Call or send for our catalog of more than 300 outdoor books published by:*

The Mountaineers
1001 SW Klickitat Way, Suite 201
Seattle, WA 98134
1-800-553-4453